BLINDSIDED
BY GOD

BLIND-SIDED BY GOD

DISAPPOINTMENT, PAIN, AND THE UNTAMABLE GOODNESS OF GOD

PETER CHIN

B E T H A N Y H O U S E P U B L I S H E R S

a division of Baker Publishing Group
Minneapolis, Minnesota

Published by Bethany House Publishers
11400 Hampshire Avenue South
Bloomington, Minnesota 55438
www.bethanyhouse.com

Bethany House Publishers is a division of
Baker Publishing Group, Grand Rapids, Michigan

Printed in the United States of America

Library of Congress Cataloging-in-Publication Data
Chin, Peter (Minister)
    Blindsided by God : disappointment, suffering, and the untamable goodness
of God / Peter Chin.
        pages cm
    Summary: "Pastor Peter Chin shares about a difficult year of his life—
burglaries, a failed church plant, and his wife's breast cancer—to encourage
those seeking understanding and hope in the midst of suffering"—Provided by
publisher.
    ISBN 978-0-7642-1292-5 (pbk. : alk. paper)
    1. Suffering—Religious aspects—Christianity. I. Title.
    BV4909.C45 2015
    248.8′6--dc23   2014041609

Cover design by LOOK Design Studio

15 16 17 18 19 20 21   7 6 5 4 3 2 1

● ● ●

To my wife, Carol, and to our children,
Sophia, Katie, Jonathan, Lucy, and Xavier.

A seventy-thousand-word book might seem like a lot,
but it doesn't even begin to describe
how precious you all are to me.

● ● ●

Contents

Acknowledgments   9

Introduction   11

1. It's *Aspen*, Not Old Spice   19
2. Prepare to Be Broken   37
3. Welcome to the Neighborhood   51
4. "It's Cancer"   67
5. A Drop in Coverage   83
6. Triple Negative   97
7. "He's Up to Something"   111
8. "I Don't"   125
9. The Seminary of Suffering   141
10. The Mulberry and the Wisteria   159
11. A (Minor) Miracle   177
12. Nothing Can Hinder the Lord From Saving   191
13. Not Just Higher—*Better*   209

Epilogue: "What About My Happy Ending?"   223

Acknowledgments

A huge thank you to my editor, Andy McGuire at Bethany House, as well as Jeff Braun. You believed in this book before anyone else did, and held to that conviction even when I was prepared to give up. This book would not exist had it not been for your faith.

Thank you to the congregations I have served over the past few years: Riverside Covenant Church of Washington, D.C., Peace Fellowship Church of Washington, D.C., and Rainier Avenue Church of Seattle. I will always be more of a pastor than a writer, and serving you has brought me deep joy and kept me grounded. Although it may not seem like it, this story is very much your story as well.

Thank you to the ministries and individuals who have helped me gain some sort of platform from which to share my experiences: *Christianity Today*, *RELEVANT Magazine*, the *Washington Post*, NPR's *Tell Me More*, and *CBS Sunday Morning*—more specifically, Katelyn Beaty of *Christianity Today*, Michel

Martin of NPR, and Sari Aviv of CBS. You helped this completely unknown pastor become, well, slightly better known.

Thank you to all the people who believed in me when I did not believe in myself, who kept on encouraging me through repeated rejections and disappointments—there are too many of you to name here. I would have never made it this far had it not been for your kind words and exhortations.

Lastly, thank you to my family. To my incredible wife, Carol, heart of my own heart and my personal hero. To my children, Sophia, Katie, Jonathan, Lucy, and Xavier. Nothing brings me more joy than to see your faces and to spend time with you all. And now that I'm finally done with this book, hopefully I can do a lot more of just that. Maybe we should go to Dutch Wonderland . . .

Introduction

Is this it? I thought to myself.

I sat in my front-row chair, elbows on my knees, pretending to be deep in thought and prayer—an old pastors' trick. In truth, I was resisting the urge to look behind me. After twenty seconds of courageous resistance, I finally succumbed and stole a glance backward at the congregation.

Oh, man, is this it? Ten people?

I took out my phone to check the time: 10:35 a.m. Well, no point in telling our praise leader that she should start late, since we were already five minutes behind schedule. And so with resignation, I rose from my position of false piety to tell her to begin our service. *Let's get this started,* I wearily thought to myself. *That way, we can just get it over with.*

Yes, sometimes even pastors feel this way about Sunday mornings.

The songs we sang that June morning in 2010 testified to the joy and hope that we have with God: *"There is joy in the*

Lord. . . . There is hope in the knowledge of Him." These were words I had sung many times before with great conviction. But not that day. My lips moved, but my attention was focused on the reality just beyond my peripheral vision: Nearly a year after planting this church, we had only ten people in attendance.

Even though I should have been thinking about God, I found myself doing something far less edifying: comparing myself to my peers. Across the country, I had half a dozen friends who had started churches around the same time I had, and they had more than ten times the number of people attending on Sundays. Their church websites were an elegant ballet of Flash animation and vintage photo filters, replete with liberal use of Helvetica font. Ours looked like it had been created in the 1990s and best viewed with Netscape Navigator. To my coldly logical mind, all of this could mean only one thing: I had failed as a church planter, and as a pastor. Perhaps even as a human being.

As the final song concluded, I plodded to the front of the small ballroom we rented to share the sermon. It was taken from a passage in Luke 7 where Jesus cares for a widow who has just lost her only son. Unlike other miracles in the Gospels, there is no great act of faith by or on behalf of this widow; she doesn't press through the crowd to touch his cloak, nor is she lowered through the roof by faithful friends. Truthfully, she does not seem to even be aware of Jesus at all. Instead, it is Jesus who takes the initiative to comfort her, not with a grand sermon, but by simply saying, "Don't cry." How comforting it is to know that in the moments we lack the strength to come to Jesus, Jesus instead comes to us.

As I shared this, I looked out at our own tiny congregation and saw that widow in many of us: a young woman who had bravely struggled with bipolar disorder since her teenage years and counted every year that she did not commit suicide as nothing short of a miracle; a refugee from Iraq raising her young son while violence consumed her home country; a couple struggling with the loss of a pregnancy, a diagnosis of cancer, and then another miscarriage.

And then my eyes fell on my wife, Carol. She held our squirming younger daughter, Katie, in her arms, while our older daughter, Sophia, sat patiently beside them. Carol was bald. We had shaved her head a few months prior, in anticipation of the chemotherapy treatments for her breast cancer. Even from across the room, I could clearly see the dark-purple circles under her eyes, signs of extreme fatigue caused by those treatments. The chemo devastated her red blood cell count and necessitated regular blood transfusions. She had scars all over: the faint one on her cheek that she had had ever since I had met her thirteen years ago, and one near her neck, from the port through which anticancer drugs were pumped into her jugular. And invisible to anyone else, the jagged scar from her mastectomy, a thin seam of pale and shiny flesh that ran half the width of her entire chest.

But what was most striking about my wife's appearance was her stomach: round and taut, heavily pregnant with our third child. Yes, she had breast cancer . . . but she was also six months' pregnant. And so my struggle with the meager attendance at our church, as pressing as it was, was not the most serious thing on my mind, not by any stretch. No, I struggled with the horrifying prospect of life without my beautiful wife, and my children without their loving mother, and fear for the health of this precious unborn child who swam in a toxic mix of chemotherapy drugs. Our church was dying, and I was failing as a pastor, but those were the least of my concerns.

I shouldn't have looked at Carol, not at that moment, and not while preaching. Because when I did, a question shot through my mind so distressing that I forgot where I was in my sermon—what

13

I was even talking about—and stood in awkward silence before my congregation of ten broken souls.

God, why are you doing this to us?

●　●　●

There are many reasons why it is important to address questions about the terrifying and difficult reality of suffering in human life. There is scarcely a discussion of Christianity that does not at some point broach this topic, and because of this, all Christians must put some thought into this issue. It simply does not do to cast about for right-sounding answers on the spot, because chances are, we will end up sharing something both unorthodox and unhelpful. This can have a devastating impact on others, especially if their faith is just at the point of beginning, or ending.

Moreover, of all people, Christians should understand suffering. From beginning to end, the pages of Scripture are filled with trials and hardships of all sorts, from the fall in the garden of Eden, to the enslavement and exile of Israel, to the persecution of the early church. We place our faith in a Savior who saved humanity through his death on a cross, and we regularly take time to remember that sacrifice through the Lord's Supper. People who count themselves as followers of the suffering Servant and descendants of a church started by martyrs should not be strangers to the discussion of suffering.

But these are not the only reasons we answer such questions, nor the most important. For some, human suffering is largely a philosophical discussion, one to be tossed around the table at Starbucks or the local pub. In that context, it's okay to agree to disagree and leave it unanswered until next time. But at some point in all our lives, we are forced to ask this question not in the third person, *but in the first.* Not "Why does humanity suffer?" but "Why do I suffer?" or "Why does someone I love suffer?" These questions are infinitely more difficult to answer, and infinitely more important.

In those moments, the subject of pain and disappointment ceases to be theological and abstract. It becomes intensely personal, connected to real people, real emotions, and real consequences. It cannot be shelved or tabled for later. It rejects simplistic or superficial explanation. It is a question we must answer, not for the sake of intellectual satisfaction, but because until we do, our lives simply do not make sense, and neither does our faith. We do not "muse" as we ask such things—we *mourn*.

And if you find yourself asking questions about suffering, not in the third person but in the first, this book was written specifically for you.

My goal is not to expound on the theological and philosophical question of the existence of suffering. There are plenty of excellent theologians and academics who can do that far better than I, and if that is what you are looking for, I encourage you to seek out their work. But let me be clear: You should read my book as well.

No, my goal is far more personal and pragmatic. If you find yourself in an especially difficult season of life, I want to plant this thought in your mind with the hope that it one day might blossom into a firm conviction:

God has not left you but is still very present in the midst of your pain.

This idea may be difficult to comprehend and contrary to how you feel, but that does not make it any less true. Thankfully, truth is hardly limited to our comprehension or feelings.

To go one step further, not only is God present in difficult seasons, but his redemptive power is such that he is even able to transform those experiences into the most blessed moments of your life. This idea may also seem to defy belief, except for the example of the cross. For if God can transform such a gruesome symbol of torture and death into one of new life and redemption, could he not do the same to the trials that you confront as well?

I also hope this book rattles your cage theologically, because in no small way, our inability to make sense of suffering is caused by some rather gross misunderstandings about the identity of God. Although we hate to admit it, our conception of God is simultaneously too narrow and too simple. He is either a benevolent grandfather who never would allow us to suffer, or he is an exacting judge who bestows suffering as a form of righteous punishment. In both of these simplistic human archetypes, either God is wrong in allowing us to suffer, or we are wrong and thus deserve our plight.

While it is true that God is both a giver of good gifts and a righteous judge, he is far more than that. He is God, and no earthly model can fully encapsulate him or his ways. God is mysterious and wild, but also loving and good. Making true sense of pain requires that we embrace both of these truths and submit to this expanded understanding of God instead of the painfully limited one we usually hold.

The question is how I want to attain such lofty goals. The most obvious answer would be to employ an equally lofty theological approach, filling this book with words no less than fifteen letters in length in an attempt to dispel any doubts as to the existence of God in the midst of suffering. But this approach would require someone a great deal sharper and more educated than I, as I hardly consider myself the most rigorous of theologians.

Instead, what I want to do is to tell you a story—the story of a year and a half of my own life, a season filled to the brim with tragedies, failures, and redemption of the most uncommon sort. It is through this perspective—that of *narrative*—that I want to explore the different aspects of suffering and the ways of God.

Don't get me wrong—as a pastor, I am obligated to do some preaching and teaching in this book. After all, I spent thousands of dollars on a seminary degree, which I have to put to some use. But for the most part I will be telling you a story—my story. It is the story of the most terrible year that my family had faced to that point, a year that began with a miscarriage, followed by a break-in, and then a frightening diagnosis of cancer. It was a year of struggle and suffering, of heartbreak and fear. It was a year in which my understanding of God was completely shattered.

But that is only half of the story, and really the lesser half.

Our story is about terrible hardship and suffering, but also providence and comfort that came through the most unexpected moments and people. It is a story about breast cancer of an especially aggressive sort, but also one of healing and hope of an even greater kind and an incredible miracle that unfolded over many months. It is the story of how my juvenile and imperfect faith imploded but was then rebuilt into something stronger than it had ever been before.

I feel compelled to tell our testimony, not so that I might boast about how I faced my situation with such amazing aplomb and faith, because I didn't. I faced it with something closer to naked and gibbering fear, as will soon become abundantly clear. My wife is a different story altogether, as you will never find a more courageous woman than she. In many ways, this book is my adoring fan letter to her.

Neither is this book my claim to Christian fame—first through authorship of a book, then national speaking engagements, and finally a Christian media empire! If I fade into complete obscurity after telling this story, that's fine with me. It's actually my deepest hope that this book will be published without a picture of me anywhere on its cover, but if absolutely necessary, preferably one from the late 1990s, as the last decade has not been particularly kind to me in the "cover photo" sense.

What compels me to tell this story is that at its very heart, this is a story about God. It is a testimony of how I discovered that even in the darkest and most discouraging moments of our lives, God does not abandon us. Instead, he is mysteriously and constantly at work, wending all things to the good of those who love him. This story is truly God's, and mine only in the sense that I had the opportunity to witness it firsthand.

And like any good story, ours starts at the beginning.

It's *Aspen*, Not Old Spice

I fell in love with Carol the first moment I saw her. But I never imagined how much pain this would eventually cause me.

My wife, an unromantic sort of woman, would deny that love at first sight is possible, but I stand by my memories of that day. It was the first Sunday of my first week at Yale, and I was visiting a small church called New Haven Korean Church, which was paradoxically located in the nearby town of Hamden and not in New Haven itself. As I walked through the front doors of this inaptly named church, there she was, handing out bulletins—a petite woman whose eyes radiated warmth and kindness, eyes I could not help but look into for much longer than what was considered polite—my future wife.

Roll your eyes or groan, if you would like. It doesn't matter to me, as I can neither see nor hear you. Nor would I care if I could, because it was hardly the only moment that demonstrates that I loved my wife from very early on. For example, not more than one month after meeting Carol, I was sitting in a dorm room with some other guys from the Christian fellowship that Carol and I both attended. At some point during the night, someone posed the question "Who do you think is the ideal woman?" which is just the Christianized version of "Who do you think is really hot?"

Everyone else needed a moment to collect their thoughts, and most likely, to separate their honest gut response from their more sanitized Christian one. I needed nothing of the sort. "Carol. Carol Bang," I immediately blurted out. They all looked at me in shock and didn't even bother to volunteer their own answers. My answer had beaten all of their own, both in speed and in depth of conviction.

The first step in my grand scheme to woo my future wife was to invite her to a dance, where my dancing skills would surely sweep her off her feet—figuratively or literally, either was fine. The afternoon of the dance, I raced home from class and with giddy excitement changed into the only suit I owned. But as I looked at myself in the mirror, I realized that the jacket and pants were mismatched shades of black. At such a tender age, I did not even know that was possible. How could black have shades? Wasn't it all just *black*?

I was horrified. Carol was surely too mature to go out with an adolescent who didn't yet own a matching suit. Or maybe I had her all wrong, that she was mature enough to see through such trivialities and recognize who I was beneath the cheap suit. Whatever the case, I wasn't going to take chances that she was more of the latter and less of the former. So to cover for my deficiency, I used cologne. Lots of it. As I left the dorm, I heard a snarky girl exclaim, "Did someone drop a bottle of Old Spice out there?!" I scoffed—it was *Aspen*, not Old Spice, you ignoramus.

Our first date (1998). It's hard to see in this photo, but my jacket and pants are mismatched shades of black.

Anxious with expectation, I arrived at the dance far too early and spent the next hour picking fretfully at my cheap, mismatched suit and checking my watch at half-minute intervals. It was nearly an hour before Carol arrived. She was simply dressed, a plain black dress with black shoes, no makeup, and her hair not made up in any way whatsoever. In fact, it looked as if she had simply put on a dress and walked out the door, a fact she confirmed to me many years later. A more perceptive person might have

21

been crestfallen, interpreting this to mean that Carol did not see this dance as a big deal in the least. But at that moment, a less perceptive person I could not have been. Smitten by love, I thought she looked positively beautiful.

We danced and twirled for hours, coughing only mildly as we parted the thin mist of Aspen cologne that trailed me everywhere I went.

Once the dance was over, I offered to walk Carol home to her dorm, which was on the opposite side of the campus. It was a bitterly cold Connecticut night, and as we passed the library, a particularly stiff wind tore across the grounds. I leapt in front of her to block her from the blast, hoping she would find this a gallant gesture, although in retrospect, it was a little silly.

It was clear that Carol saw it in that second, more foolish light, because as I marched directly in front of her, shoulders dramatically braced against the cold, she began to convulse in laughter. You might imagine this would be a painful memory for me, the prospective love of your life guffawing at your juvenile attempt at chivalry. And it would have been, except that she then grabbed my hand and pulled me to her side, clutching my arm tightly with both of her own.

I tried not to let it show too much, but this, my friends, was the best moment of my life up to that point.

A few weeks later, I asked Carol to be my girlfriend, a questionable decision given she was a senior who was going to graduate in two months and move back to Los Angeles, and I was a freshman who had three years of college remaining. But the age gap, brief time frame, and long distance didn't deter me in the slightest. She was the love of my life, and we were going to make it. And I remained absolutely certain of this fact for nearly four years, right up until I graduated from college and Carol unceremoniously dumped me for another guy.

I spent the next year in a state of deep and unrelenting depression. I struggled to accept the fact that Carol was no longer part of my life and desperately tried to purge her from my memory. I destroyed every picture I had of her, threw away every letter she had written, and gave away every present she had bought. Unfortunately, this meant that I lost the better half of my wardrobe in a single weekend.

I made feeble attempts to date other women, which went as well as you probably expect. A woman from my church set me up on a date with her daughter, and being the desperate soul I was at that time, I decided to give it a shot. I didn't have high hopes going into this encounter, but when we met in a coffee shop in New Haven, I was pleasantly surprised—my date was pretty, intelligent, and possessed a sense of humor tinged with brutal sarcasm, a trait I always found desirable despite the fact that biting wit is hardly a characteristic you want in someone you will inevitably disagree with. I was surprised to find myself attracted to her, an encouraging sign in itself given that I had a difficult time feeling any emotion except dejection.

I thought this initial attraction might blossom into something more, but it did the opposite. Our conversation, which was lively at first, became more and more halting and awkward before finally settling into an impenetrable miasma of uncomfortable silence. By the end, my attention stood fixed on the incredibly interesting half-empty coffee cup in my hands, while my date stared forlornly out the window, wondering what other hundred ways she could have better spent the last hour of her life.

Embarrassed, I apologized to her for being such a terrible date and blamed my lack of conversation on tiredness. She was kind enough to give me a sympathetic and sincere smile but paired it with a wry observation: "You know, I think you may want to consider that you're not quite over your ex just yet."

She gave my hand a pat, stood up from the table, and walked away with the slightest flick of her hair, as if to communicate what she thought of me. And she was right, of course. While hanging out with an attractive and intelligent woman, the only person I could think about was a person who was no longer thinking about me.

●　●　●

I never imagined that love and pain might be related. I always thought the two were separate, or even opposite. Love is good, suffering is bad. If someone loves you, they would never make you suffer, and if they did make you suffer, it proved that they didn't love you. If the two shared any relationship, it was one of mutual exclusivity, as if suffering was somehow the mathematical inverse of love, and the two could not coexist in the same person or the same universe.

This might seem a juvenile outlook, but it is what I had been led to believe by countless songs, movies, and TV shows—that love is a panacea, the answer to all of life's problems and ills. As John Lennon once famously wrote, "All you need is love . . . love is all you need." If John Lennon is too old for you, perhaps you have heard the song by Jason Mraz that states nearly the same thing: "All you need is love, love, lo-o-ove."

Or take the example of romantic comedies, whose plots usually include a funny but unattractive sidekick friend, as well as a breakup, a betrayal, even a minor tragedy. All of these heartbreaking situations find their conclusion in the final minutes, where the guy gets the girl (or the girl gets the guy), and they embrace in some inspiring locale, after which the screen fades to black and the credits roll. What else are you supposed to glean from this except that *love is the answer* that ties up all the messy hurts of our lives into a neat and tidy package?

It was with this same delusional mentality that I had approached my relationship with Carol. Never did I imagine that the person I loved most also held the potential to hurt me the worst. Instead, I naïvely clung to the misguided illusion that love made me invincible, when by its very nature, it did the opposite. So I developed my relationship with her to the exclusion of nearly all others, graduating from college with a photo album filled with picture after picture of Carol and me, but precious few of anyone else and me. Even worse, I made no effort to plan my life after graduation, except to move to whatever city Carol lived in. True love required nothing more.

So when Carol and I broke up, I was caught completely unaware and unprepared, like a man who steps out of a plane expecting to bask in the warmth of the Bahamas but is greeted instead by a blast of bitter arctic cold. In what seemed like an instant, I had not just lost my girlfriend, but my best friend, in many ways my only friend, as well as the past four years of my life and my plans for the future. And it was love that had positioned me so perfectly for heartbreak.

This tendency is hardly just my own, nor is it limited to romantic relationships. Whether it is with our careers, our families, our dreams, or with anyone or anything that we love, we often position ourselves for deeper and sharper pain when we pursue these things without considering how fragile the floor is beneath our feet or what would happen should that floor give way. We imagine that love will never hurt us, which is not unlike playing catch with an olive-green metal ball that has a curious circular pin attached to it. And when suffering does inevitably crash through the front door? We find ourselves traumatized, scandalized, demanding to know what it is doing here and who is to blame, not realizing that it was ultimately we who left that door unlocked.

Seeing love and suffering as mutually exclusive also allows us to entertain an especially dangerous conception of God. When we find ourselves in the midst of a particularly difficult season of life, it is only natural to ask ourselves that most thorny of philosophical questions: How can a God who loves us allow us to suffer? After all, we reason, a loving and all-powerful God would never allow us to endure pain or hardship. But since we do suffer in life, and sometimes quite terribly, it seems that the only conclusions available to us are that God doesn't love us, or that he is not powerful . . . or that he doesn't exist. There are no other answers. Suffering precludes the existence of a good and loving God, so our faith is foolish and intellectually untenable.

At the root of this train of thought lies a familiar assumption that God cannot simultaneously love us and also permit us to suffer, or again, that suffering and love are somehow mutually exclusive. On the surface, this seems like a safe-enough assumption—after all, how could anyone who loves another allow them to suffer? But the truth is, there are many instances in which this is the case. Parents do this all the time. They allow their kids to get painful shots at the doctor. They permit a dentist to drill holes in their children's teeth to place a filling. Parents will even do the "pain inflicting" themselves, taking away their kids' privileges, grounding them, or even spanking them.

Do parents do this because they hate their children or take pleasure in their pain? Of course not! No, they love their children and want what's best for them, although what parents consider best often differs wildly from that of their progeny. God himself is no different. That is why it says in the book of Hebrews:

Endure hardship as discipline; God is treating you as his children. For what children are not disciplined by their father? If you are not disciplined—and everyone undergoes discipline—then you are not legitimate, not true sons and daughters at all. Moreover, we have all had human fathers who disciplined us and we respected them for it. How much more should we submit to the Father of spirits and live! They disciplined us for a little while as they thought best; but God disciplines us for our good, in order that we may share in his holiness. No discipline seems pleasant at the time, but painful. Later on, however, it produces a harvest of righteousness and peace for those who have been trained by it.

Hebrews 12:7–11

When we suffer, it does not necessarily mean that God does not love us or that he does not exist. God allows us to suffer because in his wisdom, he knows that the suffering is somehow necessary and even beneficial, and in his sovereignty, he is able to transform even the worst of circumstances for the good of those who love him. So if God is anything like a loving parent, which I believe he is, he certainly might allow us to suffer, all while still loving us quite deeply.

While seeming benign, even endearing, the naïve notion that suffering and love are mutually exclusive is an insidious one. It leaves us brutally unprepared for pain, and on a theological level, it falsely leads us to think that because we hurt, God must not love us. No, love and suffering will always be tied to one another. Rejection by anyone is painful enough, but never worse than when it comes at the hands of someone you care about. That is why our family makes us want to tear the hair from our heads, not because they mean nothing to us, but because they mean everything. Similarly, the grief and pain you experience when you lose someone is directly connected to what place they held in your heart. The closer to the center they resided, the greater the hole they will leave behind. So unless we want to be forever scandalized by the reality of suffering, it is vital that we jettison this assumption and accept the reality that pain and love always come hand in hand—*always*.

But fortunately, this is not the end of the relationship between love and suffering, nor was it the end of my relationship with Carol.

●　●　●

My breakup with Carol took place in the fall of 2001, at nearly the same time as 9/11 and the subsequent invasion of Afghanistan by the United States. These tragic events lent an even more catastrophic air to what I was going through personally. It seemed that there wasn't a shred of good news to be found anywhere in the world, which only compounded the deep sense of personal depression and sadness I was already experiencing.

But this was also significant because Carol had graduated from Yale with a master's degree in international public health and worked for an organization that set up emergency health facilities in war zones throughout the world: Liberia, Eritrea, Burundi, and Afghanistan. And so only months after the Twin Towers plummeted to the streets of Manhattan, she was sent into Afghanistan to make sure that medical services were available to those people who were most affected. Not only had my girlfriend dumped me, but she would be traveling to the most dangerous part of the world, where I would have little to no ability to contact her, and therefore no way of knowing if she was safe, nor any hope of salvaging our wrecked relationship. If I had any illusions about it before, they were gone now—it was over. We were over.

Or so I thought, until the summer of 2002, nearly a year after our breakup.

Carol worked six months in Afghanistan, helping to set up health services (2002).

One very early morning, I got a call on my cell phone. Groggily I picked it up and looked at the screen. I was bewildered to find it crammed with numbers. *Why are there so many numbers there? And what is area code 93?* Filled with skepticism and no small measure of ill will, I answered the phone with a curt "Hello?"

In response, a faintly British voice said to me, "Hello, is this Peeteh?"

I had never spoken to a faintly British person in my entire life, much less at five in the morning, so I didn't immediately answer yes. Instead, I very intelligently responded with " . . . What?"

"Is this Peeteh, Peeteh Chin?"

29

"Yes, yes, this is Peeteh, I mean, Peter. Who is this?"

"Peeteh, my name is Clementina, and I'm friends with Carol. We're heah in Afghaneestan togethah."

As if someone had thrown a bucket of ice water over me, I threw off my covers and jumped out of bed. But it wasn't out of excitement—it was fear. I immediately assumed the worst—that Carol had been injured or even killed in an attack, or perhaps kidnapped, and her friend was calling me to break the news. This may seem like an overreaction on my part, but it was not. In fact, only a few years after this, Clementina herself would be kidnapped at gunpoint, only to be released after a sustained outcry from the many Afghan women that she had helped.

She continued, "Anyway, I just wanted to say hi to you before I handed the phone off to Carol, and I must say, your voice sounds very sexy. Good-bye, Peeteh!"

If I harbored any resentment toward Clementina for calling me that early in the morning, it immediately evaporated when she said I had a sexy voice. It's hard to stay mad at someone so marvelously perceptive. But even more wonderful, I was going to talk to Carol for the first time in nearly a year. I had imagined this situation countless times before and had prepared exactly what I would say to her if given the chance. First, I would play it cool and say hello very casually. Then throughout our conversation, I would perfectly time all my responses so as to communicate how well I had been doing without her, but not so much that I didn't leave the door open for us to rekindle our relationship. It was a delicate balance to try to strike. But as I heard muffled voices and the rustling sounds of Clementina handing the satellite phone over to Carol, my elaborate plans were completely forgotten. All I wanted was to hear her voice and to know that she was okay. So I suppose it was strange that I gave her little chance to say anything at all.

"Hello, HELLO?? Hello, Carol?? Carol? Are you okay; are you safe? Are you calling from Afghanistan?" (I know, brilliant. But it was five in the morning.)

She laughed joyfully, the same way that she had when I walked her across the campus all those years ago. Instantly I knew something had changed. Over a scratchy and delayed satellite phone, in the heart of the most dangerous country in the world, Carol told me she had been praying for me and our relationship and realized that she had made a terrible mistake. She apologized for breaking up with me and for breaking my heart, and she asked if I ever would consider getting back together again.

Our wedding day, October 2003.

You might imagine that I hesitated at such a question. After all, Carol had dumped me for someone else and had put me through my own private hell for one year. She had made me suffer more than I had ever suffered before. But before her question could even be fully bounced off the satellite and to my ear, I had already replied. In truth, I had replied weeks and months ago: "Yes. Of course, sweetheart, of course. Of course." The answer was easy, because you will always be willing to suffer, as long as it's for someone you truly love.

● ● ●

Suffering is a surprisingly accurate expression of love, a fact my immigrant Korean parents demonstrated to me. My parents are not always easy people to get along with. Or live with. Or be related to. When I was young, what was most important to my parents was not my personal happiness or growth as a human being, but being *first*: first in school, first in tennis, first at cello. They very rarely told me that they loved me—in fact, they rarely do to this day. When I relate this to my American friends, they look at me in horror and gently pat me on the shoulder. "What a horrible way to grow up!" they murmur, tilting their heads at a particularly sympathetic angle.

While I appreciate their sympathy and head tilting, I don't really need it. Although difficult at times, I am 100 percent certain that my parents love me, because they suffered for me. In my childhood, my father owned a wholesale hat store in the West Loop of Chicago. I've heard that this neighborhood is rather nice now, known for its chic restaurants that showcase a variety of craft beers. But at that time, it was known mostly for crime. My father was robbed several times at his store. One time someone clubbed him in the head with the butt of a shotgun and then sprayed bleach directly into his eyes to expedite the getaway. To this day, when my father gets tired, his eyes take on a reddish-pink tint, a daily reminder of that experience.

When my dad's hat business closed down, the five-foot force of nature who is my mother decided to start her own furniture store, never mind that she had absolutely no experience in that field. Between them, my parents worked over a hundred hours a week in that store, assembling and delivering heavy furniture, never taking a vacation, never buying anything for themselves, although they shelled out thousands of dollars for lessons of various sorts, whatever was most likely to guarantee their children entry into an Ivy League school.

They didn't do this because they had a peculiar passion for selling hats or furniture, or staring down the barrels of shotguns. They endured these tortures solely for the sake of their children: my older sister, brother, and me. They were willing to suffer terribly because they loved us—because they wanted us to have a chance at a good life in America, go to a great college and become either a doctor or a lawyer (but certainly not a pastor), and never have to endure the life they were forced to. And so I don't need my parents to say they love me to know that it's true. Their years of sacrifice and suffering on my behalf have already made that abundantly clear.

Not coincidentally, suffering is also how we can be certain of God's love for us.

Jesus' life was similarly filled with suffering, from its beginning to its supposed end. He was born in a barn (or perhaps a cave, some scholars say), which is a pretty bad start for anyone, first century or not. But to make matters worse, the king of the Jews, Herod, wanted to kill him and was willing to massacre many other boys to do so. When Jesus grew older, he was despised by the religious authorities, who conspired to murder him. Eventually they succeeded in getting him arrested and put on trial—where he was rejected by the very people he came to save—flogged, and put to death by one of the most brutal means of execution of that time, maybe of all time: crucifixion. Christ suffered—that much is certain.

But we should never forget that this suffering had tremendous purpose. Not only did Jesus' trials achieve the forgiveness of our sins, thereby restoring our relationship to God the Father, but they also served as a profound demonstration of the depths of his love for us. That is why the apostle Paul wrote, "But God demonstrates his own love for us in this: While we were still sinners, Christ died for us" (Romans 5:8). The apostle John put it this way: "This is how we know what love is: Jesus Christ laid down his life for us" (1 John 3:16). That is what Jesus' pain was—not simply the *mechanism* through which he would pay for the sins of humanity, but also a *declaration* of his love for that same humanity: "I love you so much I am willing to suffer and die, not for my sins, but for yours."

Here lies the most damaging consequence of separating love from pain: We become blind to the depths of God's love. We Christians are people who stand in the shadow of the cross, covered in precious blood that was shed out of love for us, yet still weep bitterly because we fail to receive the cheap trinkets we so covet. We are children who live in a loving and safe home but pout most wretchedly because our parents always give us what we need, and only sometimes what we want. And this is the reason that in times of trial, we are so quick to lose faith in God's love for us—we forget that his love is exhibited most clearly not through our own pleasure, but through Jesus' pain.

While hardly a flattering portrayal, it is for the most part an accurate one of us, especially of me. I cringe to think of all the times that I doubted God's love and power, even his existence, simply because my life was not going in the direction or at the pace that I wanted. But this also means that if we can somehow accept that suffering is one of the best proofs of love that exists, we might then be able to see God's love more clearly than we have ever before.

Prepare to Be Broken

Church planting is popular nowadays, and most Christians have heard about it in one context or another. But for the uninitiated, church planting at its simplest is the act of starting a brand-new church. I became aware of it while in seminary in Los Angeles, when a pastor told me I would make an excellent church planter. I thanked him, but frankly, I had no idea what he was talking about. It's like being told you would be good at curling—that bizarre winter Olympic sport that involves sliding stones on ice. You have to go online and Google it first.

"Oh, so THAT'S what church planting is!"

But over the next few years, the more I learned about church planting, the more I wanted to do it. And by early 2009, I finally felt I was ready. I resigned from my position as the college pastor of a Korean-American church in Virginia and set out to start a new church in Washington, D.C.

The first step in this journey was to attend a church-planters' conference in California. There, I could receive some basic instruction as to what it meant to plant a church and what the process would look like. I decided to fly there with my entire family: Carol, our two daughters, Sophia and Katie, and me so that as a family we could soak in the church-planting experience. Sophia was three years old at the time, a late walker but an early talker and reader. She was in every way the prototypical first child—mild mannered, eager to please, and with an uncanny ability to overhear every private conversation Carol and I attempted to have. Katie was one and a half—one and a half years of unadulterated silliness. She hardly did anything without wiggling, whether taking a bath, watching TV, even while potty training, making it an especially messy affair.

We sat both girls down one afternoon in the living room of our townhouse and told them, "Girls, we're going to take a trip to California. Daddy and Mommy need to go to a conference so that we can learn more about starting a new church, because we feel that's what God wants us to do right now." Sophia, so eager to please, nodded her head vigorously to indicate that she understood everything we were saying. Katie, eager to imitate her sister, did the same. So we continued, "And that means you guys will be going on a plane for the first time—"

"YAAAAAAY!" shrieked Sophia.

And "YAAAAAAY!" shrieked Katie, a split second after her sister. They jumped up and ran headlong around the living room, Katie not really knowing what was going on but still elated to have a reason to wiggle with all her might. Carol and I laughed as we watched their antics, our arms around each other's shoulders. We had every reason to be happy that afternoon, including one that we did not yet share with the girls: Carol was two months' pregnant with our third child, one I secretly hoped was a boy.

The conference itself was similar to other Christian conferences I had attended: colored stage lighting, a healthy selection of songs from Chris Tomlin, and lots and lots of free books. But the centerpiece of this conference was the speakers, all highly regarded church planters who shared amazing stories of how their thousand-person churches had started with only eight people, and those eight had been family members. As they spoke, I began to imagine that one day I would be sharing my own smashing successes as a church planter at the same venue, inspiring the next generation of church planters. It was at that moment that I became convinced this was truly God's will for my life. It's funny how success stories always have a way of convincing us of such things, while failure communicates only that we must have done something terribly wrong.

But one of the speakers rudely interrupted my reverie when he dared to share a less upbeat lesson with us.

"Prepare to be broken," he intoned, an intensely cool guy with spiky hair and a leather bracelet on his arm. Actually, the bracelet was so enormous that it could hardly be called a bracelet—it was more of a gauntlet than anything else, something you could imagine a hawk landing upon. I found myself idly wondering if gauntlets and hair gel were central to the church-planting experience. If so, I would have to find a Hot Topic store later that day. He continued, "Prepare to be broken personally. Prepare for your family to be broken. Prepare for the people in your church to be broken too. Prepare . . . for *brokennessss!*" The word hung throughout the room.

These warnings made all of us shift uncomfortably in our seats, as I think they were intended to do. I nodded solemnly in response and assumed a grim expression, the patented one that all Christians are supposed to wear when talking about something serious. But in truth, my melancholy was only superficial and short lived. I honestly never stopped to ponder that speaker's words, although in retrospect, I really should have. The easiest type of wisdom to ignore is that which fails to coincide with our own plans and aspirations.

The rest of the trip was not very memorable, that is, until our flight back to Dulles. It had been a smooth one for the most part. But on our descent, we hit incredible turbulence, the likes of which I had never experienced before. It started with a single shudder, one so violent that cups fell off of people's tray tables. Before an announcement could even be made that we should fasten our seat belts, the plane began to shudder and vibrate as it was buffeted by the violently turbulent air. During one particularly terrible lurch, my stomach heaved, and I immediately grabbed the barf bag in the seat pocket in front of me, as did almost everyone else on the plane. While my nose and mouth were stuffed into the bag, I stole a glimpse at Sophia and Katie, and strangely, they were completely unperturbed. With very little experience on an airplane, they probably didn't know that this much turbulence was unusual. It's interesting how novelty can sometimes serve as a viable form of courage.

But then I looked over at Carol. I was shocked by what I saw. She was doubled over in her seat, her head nearly between her knees. By her sides, her hands clutched the armrests so tightly that her knuckles stood out like a little mountain capped in pale white. But despite her grip, her hands and arms trembled violently, as if she were trying to tear the armrests from their rivets, and she breathed in short, ragged gasps. I had never seen her like this, not on a plane, not ever. I was frightened for her and wanted to ask her if she was okay, but I just couldn't bring myself to lower the bag. I don't think it would have mattered anyway, because I know what her answer would have been: "No."

And then suddenly, mercifully, it was over. With a series of unsettling bumps, we were safely on the runway, slowing down to taxi to the gate. The pilot came on the intercom and apologized for the "chop," which I suppose is pilot-speak for "terrifyingly violent turbulence." When we finally stopped to disembark, Carol and I gingerly got out of our seats and walked with the girls toward the baggage area. My stomach had finally settled down enough for me to ask her the question I had wanted to in the plane: "Are you okay? You were shaking pretty bad in there."

"I know," she replied. She paused before continuing: "I've never done that before, ever. It felt weird, like I didn't have control over my body. Peter . . . my whole body was going numb."

I could tell that she was genuinely shaken by the experience, which shook me up in return. I immediately tried to get her mind off things. "Don't worry—we've landed and we're okay now. And the girls seem totally fine—I mean, look at them! It's like nothing happened!" I laughed awkwardly and gestured to them, as if she couldn't see them for herself.

She managed a weak smile and drew a breath. "You're right—we're okay now. Let's go get our bags." But as we wobbled on, I could sense that something was wrong, that she was still troubled by the experience. Even as we walked, an anxious expression worried her face, as if she feared that something terrible had happened and we just hadn't realized it yet.

The days that followed in the summer of 2009 were filled with preparations for the church plant, especially spending time in the city, exploring and getting to know different neighborhoods. One story from this time stands out to me. I was wandering through the city one afternoon and found myself in the Columbia Heights neighborhood. Columbia Heights was undergoing rapid development, with new condos being constructed at a frightening pace and a massive shopping center erected so quickly it was as if it had been dropped from the sky. A block away from the Metro stop, I happened upon a church building that stood on a corner lot, the grounds immaculately kept and a red For Sale sign standing on the lawn.

Now, seeing that I had no congregation and no money at that time, I had absolutely no intention of buying a church building—I was there on a total whim, nothing more. Out of curiosity, I took out my phone to call the number on the sign to ask how much the church was selling for. But before I could even finish punching in the numbers, someone tapped me on the shoulder. Now, since I lived in a sleepy Virginia suburb at that time, I was a little jittery about being tapped on the shoulder by anyone in D.C. I made a bizarre sheeplike "baaing" sound and whipped around to find an older African-American gentleman regarding me curiously. He politely asked, "Excuse me . . . are you waiting here to meet someone?"

My heart pounding and ashamed of my sheep noise, the best I could do was a halting reply. "Um . . . no. Are . . . you?"

"Oh, I saw you looking at our church's For Sale sign and thought you might be coming to meet our real estate agent."

At that point, I could have just told him no, sorry, that I was just walking around the neighborhood and would be on my way. But instead, in a moment of rare pluckiness, I told him my story, that I wanted to plant a church in D.C. and we were looking for a neighborhood to lay down our roots. As we spoke, other men came walking down the street and joined our conversation. And before I knew it, I was talking to half a dozen men—the church's entire board of elders. I didn't know it at the time, but they were all gathering at the church for their weekly leadership meeting, and it just happened to be at the exact time I had come wandering down the street. They ended up giving me the complete and unvarnished history, not just of their church, but of Columbia Heights as a whole.

They told me their congregation had been there for over fifty years, and many of them had grown up at that church as young boys. Before then, Herbert Hoover had worshiped there, their one claim to D.C. fame. But now they wanted to sell this building and reestablish themselves in Southeast D.C., clear across the city. I asked them why they wanted to move in the first place, and one man tersely explained with a single word, "Gentrification," at which everyone grimly nodded. They said they did not feel like they fit in with this neighborhood any longer—a neighborhood that had endured race riots, a hippy invasion, and drug wars, and now was being saturated with coffee shops, vegan bakeries, and men with skinny jeans riding colorful bicycles, bike locks firmly shoved into their rear pockets. They felt like they were being firmly pushed out of their home by these invaders with wispy beards. Despite the somber tone of our conversation, we were mutually encouraged by this chance encounter and prayed together that God would continue to lead both of our churches.

When I got home from that meeting, Carol was sitting at our dining table, looking concerned. The thing about my wife is that she always hides her thoughts and feelings from others because she doesn't want to be a burden or inconvenience to anyone, a trait she inherited from her mother. Carol would make an excellent poker player, and I, quite possibly, the worst ever. But this also means that if she is sitting at the kitchen table, wearing an anxious expression, you know something is wrong. Immediately concerned, I asked her what was the matter.

"I'm . . . spotting," she said. "Bleeding a little bit. It's probably nothing, but I want to get it checked out."

We drove over to the local hospital, where, coincidentally, one of our close friends, Joe, was on duty in the ER. We told Joe that Carol was a few months' pregnant but was experiencing some uterine bleeding, something that had never occurred with her previous two pregnancies. A seasoned emergency room doctor, he calmly told us he would do an ultrasound right away to see what was going on. As Carol lay down on the emergency room bed, Joe prepared the ultrasound monitor, which uses inaudible sound waves, to listen in on what was going on inside her body.

Joe swept the ultrasound probe to different areas of her stomach, one moment by the belly, one by the hip, and back to the belly. On the audio transmitter, we could hear constant static, whooshes, followed by static again. He was intently listening for something, and I strained my ears as well, although I had no idea what I was listening for.

After many minutes of this, he finally put down the probe and sat down next to us. He gently put his hand on Carol's shoulder. "Guys, I hate to tell you this," he said, "but I wasn't able to find a heartbeat with the ultrasound. Carol, I'm pretty sure you had a miscarriage."

We looked at each other and didn't say a word. Nothing like this had ever happened to us, and we didn't know how to respond. Joe continued: "I know this is hard, but I want to just tell you that this kind of thing happens all the time. All . . . the . . . time. Most women don't even know that they're pregnant before they've miscarried. It doesn't mean that you can't get pregnant again either. It's just one of those sad things that often happen during pregnancy."

In a strained voice, Carol asked, "How did this happen? Could it have been anything we did?"

"It's hard to say, really. Honestly, we don't know why some pregnancies terminate like this. It can be for genetic reasons; it can be something in the environment. But the truth is, no one knows for sure. Unless you are not taking care of yourself, or something physically traumatic has taken place recently, I wouldn't think about it too much."

When Joe said this, I immediately thought back to the plane flight, how Carol was shaking uncontrollably. Could it have been the stress of that landing? Was it possible that she was in shock on the plane, and that caused the miscarriage?

At last, Joe quietly stood up and told us that if we needed anything, to give him a call. We thanked him and stood up to leave. On our drive home, I didn't have much to say to Carol, but I figured that eventually I would have something comforting or insightful to share with her. I just needed some time to process things.

The rest of that summer was difficult for Carol. She had to adjust to the loss of the baby, a life that had been growing inside of her, which she had just started to cherish. Despite the fact that Joe had told us we could still get pregnant in the future, Carol began to give away all of our baby clothes and toys, convinced she would never get pregnant again. And then eventually, as is the case with natural miscarriage, she passed the fetus from her body, a horrific end to an already traumatic process.

Still, through all this, I had little to share with her, no words of comfort and no real understanding of what she was going through. My silence was not lost on Carol either. We got into many more disagreements than usual during this time, and during one of our dustups, she said how she felt like I didn't understand what she was going through. I was preparing a sharp retort when I realized that she was right—I *didn't* understand what she was going through. I couldn't sympathize with her, couldn't connect with her experience. I knew the miscarriage was supposed to be a big deal—I truly did. But it didn't feel like that big of a deal, not to me. And because I didn't know how I should feel, I didn't know what to say.

I know this hardly reflects well on me as a husband, or as a pastor. But in my defense, my lack of response had nothing to do with a lack of love for my wife. It does, however, speak to my general lack of experience with suffering up to that point. Sure, I had had my fair share of difficulty in life, some (much) of it self-inflicted. I had a strict childhood where a lot was expected of me, more than I was possibly able to achieve. I had had my heart broken several times by that point, which may not seem like a big deal, but for those of you who have experienced it yourself, it sure feels serious enough. And not long before then, I had lost a good college friend, who, at the age of twenty-five, died after a heroic fight against cancer.

So I had always imagined that these struggles allowed me to identify and sympathize with anyone's plight. After all, I had *suffered*. But the miscarriage was the first moment I realized that this was not at all true. I couldn't even properly console my wife as she journeyed through the loss of our own child. How could I ever have foolishly thought myself an expert on the subject of pain? There were deeper depths of suffering than I had ever experienced to that point, and I was nothing but a novice.

I've learned that we should be very, very careful before we claim authority over anything as vast and ominous as suffering.

So I take full responsibility for my lack of appropriate response to my wife's miscarriage, and to intimate anything else would be ridiculous. But at the same time, I wonder if church had something to do with it too. To my knowledge, I'd never heard miscarriage addressed in church, except in a very passing and indirect way. I have certainly never heard a sermon on it or heard a church leader share publicly about experiencing one. Neither do I remember any references to miscarriage in seminary, although I did have several discussions on supralapsarianism and other esoteric theological concepts. Miscarriage was never discussed in any of the Christian contexts in which I most commonly found myself.

The more I thought about this, the more it bothered me. After all, Joe had told us that miscarriages were common, so common that they are the reason it is suggested that you don't share about a pregnancy before a certain time, because there is still a strong chance that you might lose the baby in the first couple of months of pregnancy. I could also clearly see that miscarriages could be traumatic for women, as it was for my wife. Then why had I never heard this topic addressed in any meaningful way in any Christian setting—the church, fellowship, even in seminary, for two decades?

I think it has something to do with the word *brokenness*.

I have honestly never heard *brokenness* used outside of the Christian context. Do a Google search on the term, and the references are almost exclusively Christian, except for one to "IPv6 Brokenness," which I'm guessing has something to do with the Internet. But in Christian circles, it is a commonly used term, liberally sprinkled throughout sermons, songs, books, and Christian conferences on church planting. It is a word that describes twin ideas of tremendous spiritual significance: the process by which God refines people, but also the attitude of humility that we take before God. It is a good word.

But *brokenness* is also a euphemism. And like all euphemisms, it distances us from reality.

I have discovered that Christians have something of a love affair with euphemism. This is understandable and even warranted, as the Christian life involves theological or spiritual concepts that cannot be described in any other way. But these wonderfully poetic words can also be terribly deceptive ones, allowing us to bypass the need to mention harsh realities by name and so ignore their existence. With a knowing wink and a nod, we can talk about *fallenness* without having to talk about what *fallenness* actually entails. Incidentally, my computer's spell check function refuses to even recognize *fallenness* as a real word.

When someone tells us to prepare to be "broken," we can solemnly nod but then go our merry way, because that term, although serious in tone, is just vague enough to allow us to ignore it or at least not take it as seriously as we should, much like any other word of the Christian vernacular. It is a spiritual word that can unfortunately disconnect us with real examples of brokenness . . . that is, unless we go on to fill in the messy details that we choose to ignore:

Prepare to be broken by miscarriage or by the terminal sickness of someone you love. Prepare to be broken by mental illness. Prepare to be broken by the prospect of having a child with deep disabilities or losing that child altogether. Prepare to be stricken by doubt, both in your calling and in your ability to follow that calling. Prepare to be smashed by people's criticism and disapproval of every choice that you make, no matter how well intentioned. Prepare to be imprisoned by fear of the future, fear of failure, fear of not living up to your/others'/ God's expectations. Prepare to be broken by _____.

We so rarely bother to fill in that blank.

This always makes me think of the time I visited the Department of Justice. I don't often venture into that part of D.C., afraid as I am of being run over by oblivious tourists riding on Segways. But a friend once invited me to lunch near there, and I thought I would stop by to take a look. The walls of the DOJ are covered in huge murals, each depicting scenes from American history. One of the more striking murals, painted by John Steuart Curry, depicts a lynching. In the mural, a man holding a rope leads a mob in pursuit of a single man, flames burning in the background. And the only one standing between the mob and its prey is a judge, holding them at bay at the courthouse steps with a single upraised hand.

When you think about it, Curry could have just as easily painted a symbolic scene that included a classical blindfolded Lady Justice, holding her sword and scales, with her carved sandal stomping on a snake. But he didn't. He painted a lynching, a terrible but very real moment of failure from our history. And that way, we are not allowed to gloss over or remain disconnected from justice and its inverse. Injustice is not a theoretical idea. It is when a mob chases a man down, puts a rope around his neck, and hangs him from a tree for an assumed but unproven crime. That's injustice.

I think it's important that Christians do the same and summon up the courage to call things by their proper names. We have to stop relying so heavily upon spiritual euphemisms to describe the hardest elements of our lives and recognize that a spirit of avoidance is not always the same as the spirit of peace. This is precisely what we find in the reinstatement of the apostle Peter. After Peter denied Jesus three times on Good Friday, you would imagine that the compassionate thing for Jesus to do would be to let the whole thing slide and never mention Peter's failure again. That's what I would have wanted Jesus to do. But instead, Jesus directly and specifically reminded Peter of his failure by asking him, not once but three times, "Do you love me?" a fact that pained Peter deeply. To us, this seems unnecessarily cruel, but without this confrontation, Peter could not be forgiven and restored, and would never become the disciple that he was destined to be. True restoration demands that we travel through pain, not simply around it.

Similarly, we need to say the words *miscarriage, abortion, mental illness,* and *drug addiction,* not for the shock value those words hold, but so that we can look our issues straight in the face and deal with them directly and more effectively, and without shame. If we do not, and instead content ourselves only with speaking euphemistically, we leave people dreadfully unprepared for the reality of life and forego the true restoration God desires for us.

But I don't want to go too far in my criticism of the church. Surely not every church avoids such discussions. Like I said earlier, regardless of whether the church had taught me anything about it or not, the responsibility was on me as a husband to listen to Carol and figure out how best to support her. That was my job, my responsibility, and not the church's. Still, there are some moments when it doesn't matter how direct or honest you are about suffering, because nothing will prepare you for the enormity of what you face. Although words of wisdom are helpful, some things you just have to experience firsthand to have any conception of how frightening they are.

3

Welcome to the Neighborhood

Please initial here, here, and here, and sign here," the lawyer said for the fifteenth time. It was September 2009, and we were at our Realtor's office, closing on a wonderful single family home in Northeast D.C. By that point in the signing process, my signature had devolved into something completely unlike its usual self. It looked like the signature of a person who didn't really know cursive but was committed to faking it anyway. It could have been the signature for Peter Chin, but just as easily, Pratnesh Singh. Part of the reason it had devolved so terribly was the number of times I had to sign my name. But partly it was because a camera crew from a local PBS affiliate was filming us for a segment on real estate, and my signature just couldn't handle the pressure of being on camera.

The house was something of a miracle for us: located not too far from the neighborhood where we wanted to plant the church, with plenty of space for our family, including a basement and yard for Sophia and Katie to play in. We were giddy at the prospect of finally closing on the house and moving in.

" . . . Here, and here, here, and here . . . aaaand here. We're done! Congratulations. You guys are now homeowners!"

Our real estate agent handed us a bottle of champagne, and together, Carol and I turned and beamed into the video cameras, my smile as forced and affected as my signature had become. But no small percentage of that smile was genuine, as I was excited to open the door to our new home and begin our new life.

On the way to the house, we excitedly discussed what color we should paint the rooms and whether we should install new faucets. We continued to talk about these things as I opened the front door and took a step inside, when I sensed something was wrong. I looked around and saw a few Realtors' business cards scattered on the counter. The kitchen cabinet doors were slightly ajar, which I assumed was the work of our overzealous house inspector. But then I saw the sink, or more exactly the cabinet beneath the sink, which stood wide open. Water slowly dripped from the cabinet and was collecting in a brownish puddle on the floor. I stooped down to take a closer look and discovered the garbage disposal had been disconnected from the drain and removed altogether. And then it finally dawned on me: Someone had robbed our house. My meager street sense finally kicked in, and I told Carol to wait in the car while I checked things out.

The rest of the home was in similar condition. Nearly all of the sinks and toilets had been taken out of the bathrooms, as well as the ceiling fans in all of the bedrooms. Junk food lay strewn about the house, some of it in the most random of locations, like a pile of chicken bones I discovered in the spare bedroom closet and a bag of Doritos folded neatly in a cupboard. Most perplexing were the kids' toys scattered throughout the house—a football on the kitchen counter, a pair of foldable scooters

Burglars hit our new home in Washington, D.C., before we even moved in. They took bathroom sinks, toilets, ceiling fans, and other furnishings.

leaning on the wall by the back door. In any other situation, these would have been something of a homey sight, had it not been for the fact that none of those items belonged to us.

The police officer who came to take our report seemed anything but surprised. With a nonchalant air, he told me that property crime was rampant in the community, especially kids breaking into vacant houses. From my point of view, our home had been broken into and violated, but to him, this was no more serious than a lost dog or traffic accident. He must have sensed my incredulity, because he lowered his reflective cop sunglasses and leveled with me. "Listen, this kind of thing happens all the time around here. So, welcome to the neighborhood!" he concluded with an ironic sort of laugh. He meant that last sentence as a jest of sorts, ostensibly to set my mind at ease. But it struck a chord with me. This had become my family's welcome to the neighborhood. Before we had even owned the house for ten minutes, it had already been broken into, and anything of any value had been stolen.

●   ●   ●

Our new neighborhood was called Langdon, which lies on the far eastern border of the city. For the most part, Langdon is a quiet working-class community, lined with old crooked trees and large bungalows, and whose residents are predominantly African American. As was the case across the city, gentrification was taking place in Langdon, but not nearly at the same pace as other neighborhoods. This meant it retained much of the character of what remains of Chocolate City, as it's affectionately called by many black residents. There were small convenience shops and storefront churches, hair salons, fried chicken stores, and people crossing the street at odd locations and intervals. And of course, unrelenting crime, both petty and not so petty.

Despite our rather rude introduction, Carol and I quickly began to appreciate our neighborhood. In particular, we loved how friendly everyone was. In the suburbs, people took offense if you said hello to them. It was as if you were breaking some unspoken suburban protocol, or such an action was prohibited by the homeowners' association, which is not hard to believe. But folks in Langdon believed the opposite. They thought it rude when someone did not say hello to their neighbors, which Carol and I found refreshing. We learned to unfailingly say hello to every person who passed by, no matter if we knew them well or not. If we didn't, we were at risk of being called "un-neighborly" behind our backs, an insult of the highest degree.

We also sent Sophia to the local D.C. public school, only three blocks from our house. Sophia was one of only a handful of nonblack students, and the only Asian. At first, I had no small amount of trepidation about sending her there, afraid that she would be picked on for being different from everyone else. But that wasn't at all the case. She came home every day with a cheery attitude and nothing but positive things to say about her teachers and classmates. One night, only a few months into the school year, I was shocked and delighted when Sophia read *Go, Dog. Go!* to me, not from memory but by sight. Her teacher, Mrs. Stevens, had taught her how to read in just a few short weeks. And so Carol and I began to fall in love with this friendly little neighborhood.

But it wasn't long before the incidents started up again. One night Carol forgot to lock our car door, and the next morning, we found our minivan ransacked so completely it was as if the thief was trying to clean the car and had forgotten to put everything back. Another night I left my daughters' scooters on our front porch, newly purchased for their birthdays. In the morning, they were gone. Fortunately, a generous friend of mine felt sorry for us and bought us replacements, which I locked up in a mess of cables and locks so complicated and entangled that my daughters hardly used them. It was just not worth the hassle.

While these occurrences were maddeningly frustrating, they didn't surprise us. We knew there were poverty and unemployment in the neighborhood, and so knew that there would be petty theft. So it wasn't difficult to make some sense of these instances and put them behind us—that is, until someone stole something from us that made no sense at all.

Carol and I were doing yard work one afternoon when I noticed that she was pacing back and forth on our front porch, looking about in consternation. Finally, she called out to me, "Peter, I can't find my clogs—have you seen them?"

"No, I haven't. Where did you see them last?"

"I always put them right here on the porch, next to the front door. But I can't find them anywhere now."

I should explain that these clogs weren't the nice kind that someone would want to steal, if there is indeed such a thing. No, they were old, cracked, and looked as if they smelled terrible, although they didn't. With this in mind, I condescendingly replied, "Sweetheart, you must have misplaced them. No one wants your dirty old clogs." I caught a raised eyebrow and so quickly added, "But that's really too bad you can't find them, because you've had them for so, *so* long. I'll keep a look out for them." But even as I said this, I knew it was highly unlikely that she had misplaced them. Carol has something close to a photographic memory when it comes to the location of items.

Later that week, I was walking in a nearby park with Sophia when I saw something brown and smelly-looking over by the swings. *No, it couldn't be,* I thought to myself. Incredulous, I came in for a closer look, and my suspicions were confirmed. There they were: my wife's clogs. Someone had whisked them off of our front porch and transported them here, blocks away from our home. Sophia saw them as well and excitedly said, "Daddy, Mommy's shoes! Let's bring them back to her," running over to pick them up.

"NO!" I shouted, louder than I wanted to. I had no idea where those clogs had been since they had left our property, and frankly, I didn't want to. More gently this time, I said, "No, let's just leave them right where they are."

Sophia must have sensed my mild revulsion, because she backed away slowly from the shoes, as if they were a mess a dog had left behind. But as we left the park and the clogs behind, Sophia quietly posed a question to me that I would never forget: "Daddy, why do people always steal from us?"

Her question stunned me. I had no idea how to respond. But I wondered if I should share with her a suspicion that had been growing in the back of my mind, that perhaps race had something to do with it. Langdon is a predominantly African-American community, over 90 percent. Being a nonblack family in Langdon automatically made us a racial minority, and it is the universal fear of all minorities everywhere that they are going to be targeted for one thing or another. But we weren't just any minority—we were Korean.

Korean and African-American people in the inner city share a long and conflicted history, one too knotty and complex to try to unravel in this book. But the conflict centers around the tense relationship between Korean shop owners and African-American residents, a conflict that was on full and explosive display during the Los Angeles riots of 1994. This dynamic is largely unknown to most Americans, partly because it has broken into the public consciousness only in various and irregular moments, and partly because race is so often framed as solely a white and black thing. But most African Americans and Korean Americans are aware of this tension, even if, thankfully, not everyone buys in to it.

With all the previous thefts, I had successfully resisted this train of thought. But when someone stole Carol's clogs, a crime whose motivation smacked more of malice than any kind of financial gain, I began to fear that we were being singled out and specifically targeted for crime, not for financial reasons, but for racial ones. No, there was no specific reason that I felt this way. No person had ever come up to me and called me a slur or informed me he was going to steal from me because of my race. But I could not help but fear that this might be the case, that perhaps the answer to Sophia's question was that people stole from us because we were Korean, and Koreans and blacks just can't get along.

In the end, I decided not to tell Sophia any of this. First off, I didn't even know if it was true, that the clogs had been stolen for that reason. But more important, I didn't want *my* suspicion to become *her* reality, a fear that she had subconsciously inherited from her father. Instead, after a moment's hesitation, I gently said to her, "Well . . . there's nothing that was stolen that we can't replace," which was true. Still, the spark had been struck in my mind; all it needed now was a little fuel.

● ● ●

To stop people from stealing scooters, shoes, and other sundry items from my porch, I installed motion sensors all around the perimeter of our home, which would alert me if anyone was sneaking around. The sensors beeped all the time, several times a week, and sometimes several times a night. Every time they did, I would peer through the window blinds and inevitably see a cat or raccoon scurrying off into the distance—except one night, when I saw something else entirely.

That particular evening, after hearing the motion sensor go off, I looked out of our second-story bedroom window, down into our backyard. And there I saw two men hunched over by my motorized scooter, furiously trying to saw through the lock attached to its wheel. The smaller of the two thieves, who couldn't have been any more than twelve or thirteen, looked around nervously. At one point, spooked by some sound he heard on the street, he stood up and flattened himself against my backyard fence, his head swiveling from the right to the left, looking for all the world like the Pink Panther from the old 1960s cartoons.

The other man was more focused. As he was stooped over with his back facing me, I couldn't see his face. But his tank top revealed his broad shoulders and powerfully muscled back, the frame of someone who lifted a lot of weights. He was working quickly but patiently, undeterred by the minor street noise that had startled his smaller collaborator. He clearly had done this before.

I left the window, scrambled for my phone, and called the police. In a hushed whisper, I told them that two men were in my backyard, trying to steal my scooter. The operator told me they would send a car as soon as they could, but it might take a while because things were so crazy in the city that night.

I said that was fine. I figured it would take no more than ten minutes for the cops to show up. As I waited, I peeked out the window to keep tabs on the thieves. They were having a harder time than they probably had anticipated. My scooter was locked with a heavy-duty chain, which was attached to a steel shackle that I had buried in a solid foot of concrete. I think they had a little hacksaw, which just wasn't going to cut it, literally. It was going to take them a long time to get anywhere.

Thirty minutes later, I was still waiting for the police. The smaller thief was losing interest and was poking at something on the ground, while the larger one was starting to lose steam, his shirt soaked in sweat, shoulders glistening from the effort. "No, no, no," I said to myself, frantically redialing 9-1-1. I didn't want them to leave just yet, not until the cops came and threw them up on the hood of their car and talked some sense into them. I made my report to the operator again, telling them I had already been waiting half an hour for an officer to come. The operator was apologetic but said, "It's a crazy night here. I have to tell you . . . I don't think there will be a squad car available for at least fifteen more minutes."

I shook my head. *A forty-five-minute police response time to a 9-1-1 call? Ridiculous!* I looked back out the window, and the boys had already jumped my fence and left, realizing they would need more than a hacksaw to cut through a hardened steel shackle. There was no point in having an officer come out now just to take a useless report. I told the operator to cancel the call, at which she sounded relieved.

I didn't sleep for the rest of that night. I spent most of the night planted by my bedroom window, periodically peering down into my yard to see if the crooks had returned and half hoping they would so that I could teach them a lesson. And as I stared glumly into the darkness, I became convinced that we were indeed being singled out for crime. But it was not because I owned a scooter and not because people were poor or unemployed. It was my race. No one else was going through this kind of ridiculousness except for my family and me. People felt free to steal from us because we were different, because we were Korean. And I honestly wondered if it wasn't too early to sell the house and move out, only months after having moved in.

I spent most of the morning after the attempted scooter theft outside, re-securing my scooter and other possessions that I stored outdoors. I glumly wondered if I should chain my sandals to the porch to prevent them from being purloined as well. As I crossly tramped through my yard, I saw my neighbor across the street, a Jamaican man I had not yet had the opportunity to meet at length. We fell into a conversation, and I told him about the scooter and how my kids' stuff had been stolen earlier. He shook his head. "I bet I know those kids. Tall one and a short one, right? Tall guy built like a truck?" Amazed, I nodded my head. "They took my son's bike off our porch last month. His little friend even had the gall to ride it around the neighborhood afterward, in plain sight!"

I told him I was sorry, but the fact was, this news actually made me feel a lot better. Not that his stuff had been stolen—that would have been misanthropic, if not downright "un-neighborly" of me. No, I felt better because it dawned on me that I wasn't the only one going through this. My neighbor was going through the same situation as I was, and he was black. Relieved, I told him I would be looking out for his house, and he said he would do the same for me. It was nice to know I was not alone and that someone had my back.

As I continued to work outside my house, another neighbor passed by, one who had lived on our block since the 1960s. Still feeling more than a little sorry for myself, I repeated my story about the two boys who had tried to steal my scooter. I thought I would get sympathy but instead received home security advice that I had never heard before.

"Have you tried bear traps?" he asked.

"Excuse me?"

"Bear traps. Kids were always coming into my yard, taking stuff, so I put a bear trap out there. Even caught one of them once, and they never came back after that."

"You didn't say 'bear traps,' did you?"

He looked me dead in the eye and nodded in the affirmative.

Nonplussed, I said, "Hmm, I honestly never thought of that." (*Probably because that's insane,* I thought to myself.) "Where . . . where did you get a bear trap, anyway?"

"eBay," he deadpanned.

As we continued to talk, he explained that as bad as things were, they were a hundred times worse in the 1980s, when gangs ruled the neighborhood, drug wars raged on D.C.'s streets, and five hundred people were killed every year. I found this comforting as well—again, not that drug wars had once raged in the neighborhood, but that the crime I was experiencing wasn't centered around me or my race but predated me by decades. In fact, to hear him say it, things were actually improving. My mood improved mildly as well.

Finally satisfied that every item of even minor value was secure, I headed inside for a break. I opened the local section of the *Washington Post* and discovered that the 9-1-1 operator had not been exaggerating—the previous night had been an especially tragic one in the city. In a brutal spate of violence, multiple people had been shot around D.C., and a young college student killed. The reason the police couldn't get an officer to come out to my house was because they were all scrambling to other locations around the city. And my call was probably one of hundreds relatively low in priority that night.

And then I understood. If anything, I should be thankful because I could have been calling the police for a far worse reason than some kids trying to steal my scooter. I could have been calling them because a bullet had gone through my window or through one of my children—a reality that many in the city lived with daily. Thank God it was only my scooter and not something much worse. Crime was not just my reality, but one shared by many in D.C., and a reality that existed far before my family and I had ever moved into this terrible and wonderful city.

I know. It was rather foolish of me to assume I was being singled out for crime. After all, on my very first day in the house, the police officer had warned me that property crime was rampant in the neighborhood. And given that Langdon is predominantly an African-American community, it implied that most of the victims of these crimes were black, not Korean. It was an unfair and selfish assumption for me to make.

But perhaps I should not be so hard on myself, because one of the most insidious side effects of suffering is the way it isolates us from others. The experience of pain makes us instinctively pull away from people, to be by ourselves to lick our wounds. Whether this stems from some primal sense of self-protection— as if when we are alone, no one can hurt us—or the conviction that no one else can relate to what we are going through, we tend to physically withdraw from those around us.

To make matters worse, physical isolation lends itself to emotional isolation. As we pull away from our neighbors, coworkers, and friends, it is easy to look at their lives from afar and jump to the conclusion that they don't have it nearly as bad as we do. At least, that's how things look to us from a distance, so we assume it is truth. That assumption then forces us to ask brooding questions like, "Why am I going through this and not him? What did I do to deserve this?" Or in my case, "Why do people steal from us and not my neighbors?" These questions never have satisfactory answers, and their intensely introspective nature only deepens the profound isolation that we already feel. In the end, we feel physically, emotionally, and utterly alone.

This is precisely what happened to me. With every instance of theft and crime, I developed a worsening case of fortress mentality. And in an attempt to protect myself and those I loved, I began to edge further and further away from others. Everyone who was not biologically related to me was to be viewed with the utmost suspicion: random people walking down the street, people who drove too slowly as they passed by my house, even my own neighbors. And from my distant vantage point, peering suspiciously through my blinds, it was easy to assume that none of those people had to endure what I did, that I alone was being singled out. In the dark confines of my house and the darker confines of my mind, it was easy to jump to the conclusions I did . . . until I got out of my house and actually talked to my neighbors.

It took no more than a single hour of conversation with them to realize how foolish it was to imagine that I alone was being targeted for crime. We all were, regardless of race. But it is all too easy to jump to false conclusions when you make them alone in the dark.

This principle makes me think of the prodigal son. In case you don't know the story, here's a quick summary: There's this son, and he's a jerk. He takes his share of his father's inheritance early and leaves to go party in the big city. He has a grand old time until he runs out of money, which in the circles he ran with also meant that he had run out of friends. And when a famine sweeps the land, no one is willing to take care of fun boy. By the end, he is a lowly servant, so hungry he yearns to eat slop out of a pig trough.

While starving in a pigpen, many miles away from his father, the son plans his return home. But what is striking to me is the son's perception of his father. You would assume that having lived his entire life with his father, he should know his dad pretty well. The son believes his father is an angry man and will feel nothing but rage at his return. He seems certain his father is not generous or forgiving, so his best bet is to be reinstated as a servant, and nothing more.

But as he draws closer to home, we see that the reality could not be further from the son's perception. The father is not angry. Rather, he has been anxiously scanning the horizon for his son's arrival and runs to him while he is still a far ways off. The father does not berate him but is filled with love and compassion and throws his arms around him. The father does not relegate his son to servanthood, but instead, he insists that a party be thrown for him and a ring placed on his finger and a fattened calf prepared in his honor. Most importantly, through all of this, the son sees himself clearly in turn. He is not the profligate failure that he thought himself to be, but a beloved child, and always will be.

There is a reason the son misjudged his father so completely: You can never see someone else clearly from the depths of a pit. When we are alone, suffering, or in a pigsty of one sort or another, it is so easy to make woefully inaccurate assumptions about our own situation, as well as the situations and motivations of others. We become convinced that no one has it as bad as we do, and no one cares. But when we draw closer to people, as the prodigal son did to his father, we see others more clearly, and ourselves more clearly in turn. Assumptions and misperceptions vanish, and the truth becomes more apparent.

The truth of suffering is this: Hardship and pain do not make us more alone in life, but less.

There is a type of fellowship that all co-sufferers share with one another, a kind of camaraderie not founded on blood, marriage, or common interest, but on pain. Because we cannot imagine that any good thing might come from pain, we are quick to write off this kind of fellowship, when in fact, some of the strongest relationships humans can have with one another are those forged through suffering.

Take, for example, the kinship shared by veterans. Everyone would agree that marriage is one of the strongest bonds any two people can share. But veterans often say that the relationship they share with their fellow soldiers, a relationship forged in foxholes and war zones, is as intense and as enduring as the bond they share with their spouse, although obviously different in character. There is a sort of fellowship that those who have suffered share with one another, a fellowship that few expect and no one ever volunteers to join, but as enduring as even the most intimate relationship that humans can enjoy.

What's more, suffering even binds us more closely to Christ. In Hebrews 2, it says that Jesus was perfected through suffering, and as a result, we are "of the same family" with Christ (verse 11). Jesus calls us his brothers and sisters. The passage even goes one step further, saying that Jesus sings our praises, like a man who boasts loudly about his siblings! What a remarkable idea, that because Jesus suffered as we do, we share a kinship with him, the same sort that veterans or survivors of any kind share. So even though we may feel very different from each other, we are never alone when we suffer—we always have our fellow sufferers, but much more than that, we have Christ himself!

To some, this doesn't sound like much—to realize that others are suffering as much as we are. After all, the fact that other people suffer does not by itself eliminate our own suffering, as if a cut on the hand of another somehow cancels out the pain we feel (unless that hand is that of Christ!). And in my own case, the fact that all my neighbors had to put up with crime did not make crime less of a reality for me, simply a shared one. While this might be true, we should not be too quick to write this off. A shared reality is infinitely better than one you shoulder alone, and finding small comfort is far better than finding none at all.

"It's Cancer"

My first exposure to the ravages of breast cancer was not through an experience with my family or a friend, but in traffic. It was the summer of 1999, and I was driving my 1988 Toyota Cressida from campus to lead a Bible study for the youth group at the church I attended. The traffic was especially terrible that day, inexplicably grinding to a complete halt only a few blocks into my drive. As is my custom in such situations, I railed and pounded the steering wheel, all but certain the traffic was caused by one simple fact: that everyone in the world is a worse driver than I am, an opinion I hold to this day.

But as we crept forward, I could see that the traffic wasn't caused by a driver's incompetence or an accident, but that a charity run was taking place on the road ahead of us. Brightly dressed runners crossed the intersection, many of them not necessarily running but happily shuffling along in the painfully nonathletic way charity runners do. Their official race-day T-shirts and hats were adorned with red ribbons, marking that they were running/ shuffling to raise money in the fight against HIV/AIDS.

Because of this, and the fact that it was such a marvelous summer day, most of the drivers around me seemed to be remarkably good-natured about the delay. Some even clapped and shouted encouragement to the runners through their open windows, which the runners gratefully acknowledged with a cheery wave of their hands and panting, openmouthed smiles. I myself had never been a part of a charity run like this and was touched by the attitudes on display, not only of the runners, but especially of the drivers. Drivers in Connecticut usually responded to traffic with wrath, the intensity of which would make even God raise his eyebrows in astonishment.

The woman in the car next to mine was yelling out her window too, but the tone of her voice was distinctly different from the others, edged with sharpness. At first, I couldn't make out exactly what she was saying, but she was clearly upset, probably because she was in a rush to get somewhere. But out of curiosity, I listened more carefully and heard her shout, "AIDS is a preventable disease! AIDS is a preventable disease!" I was stunned. She was yelling discouragements at the people who were running the race.

Disgusted and outraged, I lunged to the passenger side of my car to roll down my window and bellowed at her, "What is your problem? They're doing this for *charity*!" The woman spun to look at me, a shocked expression on her face, and then immediately turned and looked straight out her windshield, as if ashamed of what she had said or maybe just that she had been caught saying it. She refused to make eye contact with me, but with a trembling voice ragged with both anger and sadness, she retorted, "AIDS is preventable. *Breast cancer is not.*" And with that, she closed her window.

My mind and tongue wrestled each other for control as I tried to comprehend her logic—why breast cancer was of such high priority to her that she felt it necessary to criticize those who supported any other cause. Initially, I assumed the worst of her. She must still hold on to the antiquated notion that AIDS was only a gay person's disease or that AIDS victims were just suffering the consequences of their own choices. Or maybe she was one of those especially wrathful people you read about on the news who could be driven to murderous rage by traffic, willing to end all life on earth after being cut off on the road. In that moment, there didn't seem to be any other possible explanation for someone saying something so utterly vile and so lacking in perspective.

But as I continued to stare at her in disbelief, I noticed something I had not before: her hair. Something about her hair was just not right. It appeared imbalanced in some way, as if skewed a little too far to one side, hair too thick and matted and sitting too low on her brow. Speaking of her brow, she had virtually no eyebrows, except two pitifully thin lines that appeared to have been clumsily painted on with eyebrow pencil. And even though her cheeks were flushed with anger and shame after our exchange, I could still tell that she was pale and gaunt. It finally hit me: This woman had breast cancer. She must have been undergoing chemotherapy and had lost all her hair, a fact she hid by wearing a wig and makeup. As this realization dawned upon me, she began to cry, tears silently streaming down her thin face.

This was my first exposure to breast cancer. And what I gleaned from that brief encounter was that breast cancer must be *terrible*. It disfigured you, not just in body, but in heart, and transformed you into a person whose every word betrayed the terrible pain that racked both body and soul. From that moment on, the prospect of breast cancer deeply frightened me. I was relieved I would never get it, and neither would anyone I loved.

● ● ●

Fast-forward a full decade to late November of 2009. My family and I had cleared our house of all the chicken bones left by the squatters and were quickly settling into our new life in the city, stolen clogs and all. That also meant we could finally get started with this church plant in earnest, the main reason we had moved to D.C. in the first place. And all initial signs pointed to this church becoming a solid success.

The first sign that this was the case was not an external one, but the personal transformation that took place in me. I am not by nature a sociable person. In fact, whatever animal represents the opposite of a social butterfly, that is me. A forever scowling, butterfly-eating bird of some sort. But for those few weeks in the fall of 2009, I put my intense social awkwardness behind me and approached everyone I knew, and everyone that those people knew, about the church. It didn't really matter who they were or their religious background. They could have been Anglican, Pentecostal, nondenominational, Buddhist—in my mind, I was just inviting them to participate in something great that God was doing in the city and so had no reason to be embarrassed about my forwardness. To my surprise, a good number of them responded yes, that they did want to get involved. Such responses always caught me off guard because I had always assumed that their answer would be no, followed by mocking laughter and finger-pointing.

I think I may have watched too much Charlie Brown when I was young.

Eventually, the reverse began to take place, where people I barely knew were reaching out to me, asking me about our church's vision and mission. I paused, trying to remember how a vision and mission were different from one another, before deciding that it really didn't matter. I told them our church wanted to strike a balance between fostering our own personal identity as God's beloved children, as well as loving service to the surrounding community, a balance I described as "Being filled by God—overflowing to others." Through those conversations, I discovered that this sense of balance between identity and calling had deep resonance with people, many of whom were tired of churches focusing on one dynamic at the expense of the other instead of seeing them as two sides of a single coin. Eventually even clerks at grocery stores and people walking their dogs approached me to ask when and where our church met and how they could get involved. The future was bright.

Just one final unexpected obstacle stood in our way: a small lump in Carol's right breast. The discovery of this lump alarmed us, but not excessively. We were optimistic it would end up being nothing serious. After all, Carol was young and healthy and had no history of breast cancer in her family. It is fairly common for women to have a benign mass in their breast tissue. And to top it off, we were doing God's good work and planting a brand-new congregation in the city. It would make no sense for God to let Carol get sick now, of all times.

But knowing it was better to be safe than sorry, Carol dutifully went to her doctor's office in Virginia to have a mammogram. We were all but certain the doctor would confirm that the lump was nothing to be worried about, and that would be the end of it. Much to our surprise, that is not what the doctor said. Instead, he told Carol that he did not like the look of the results and wanted her to have a biopsy to make sure everything was okay.

Up to that point in our lives, both of us had been blessed with good physical health and had never heard a doctor say anything

71

to us except, "You'll be fine; be sure to exercise and eat healthy." To hear him say something different rattled us. For the first time, I began to wonder, *Could that lump be something more?* An unsettling feeling of anxiety crept into my thoughts, springing to life every time I laughed or otherwise tried to enjoy myself. I could be working on a sermon or playing with my daughters when suddenly I would find myself asking, *Could the lump be something more?* I tried again and again to push this question aside, reassuring myself by using the same arguments that I had before, but to no avail. The thought stubbornly persisted.

Eventually Carol did have her biopsy and was told to come in to the office in Virginia to discuss her results with a doctor. What I remember from that particular day was that I should have given her a hug before she left.

I don't have a very good memory at all for details. I often wander from room to room of my house, furrowing my brow as I try to remember why I came upstairs and now inexplicably find myself in the children's bedroom. And so the exact details of the day Carol went to see her doctor about the results from her biopsy are a little vague. I don't remember what I ate or what Carol was wearing or the weather that morning.

I do have a great memory for emotions, however. Details of an event may quickly pass out of mind, but I always retain an accurate memory of what I was feeling at that moment, and I can usually piece things together from there. What I remember of that day was that there was a bit of tension in the air, and I'm pretty sure it was my fault. I had stayed up too late the night before playing video games. That may not sound like that big of a deal or a cause for tension, at least for unmarried people, but married people with children know differently. After a video game binge, I am a zombie for the next twenty-four hours and nothing but a liability at home, instead of being just the minor annoyance I typically am. Carol gets annoyed with me because of this, and as a result, I get annoyed with her that she is annoyed with me, which she finds annoying in turn, if not slightly galling.

So that is all I remember from that day: She was leaving for her appointment, and things were a little tense between us. As she left, in an unnaturally stiff tone of voice, she called out, "I'm going now," and then hung there in the doorway. By her voice and delay, I knew she wanted a hug for encouragement. And I knew that I should give her that hug . . . along with an abject apology for being stupid and immature. But with the ridiculous self-righteousness that only the truly guilty dare possess, I didn't.

To some degree, I just assumed the appointment would go well. She would come home in a few hours, and everything would be back to normal. There was no need to make a big deal of this. But I did this mostly because I have this terrible habit where in the moments I know I am most wrong, I act instead as if I am most right. It's as though somehow my moral outrage alone will convince others, and perhaps even myself, that I am actually the one who has the higher ground, despite obvious signs otherwise. I have since come to realize that moral outrage has little, if anything, to do with actual morality.

So even though deep in my heart I knew it was the right thing to do, I didn't give Carol her usual hug out the door. Instead, I sullenly called out, "Bye," and that was it. She waited a moment longer, and then without a word, she closed the door behind her. *Maybe that will teach her for making me feel bad for doing something I shouldn't have been doing.*

For the next few hours, I tried to further convince myself of the rightness of my cause—that I was a grown man who worked hard for God and for his family and deserved a video game binge here and there. *Who is she to tell me what to do, like I was a child!* But it was no use—even in the twisted gravity of my mind, all my justifications fell flat, and I had to finally admit that I had screwed up royally. So I resolved to apologize to Carol at the first possible opportunity. As soon as she came home, I would give her that hug, plus an apology.

Almost as if on cue, Carol called me on the phone right then. I opened my mouth to apologize to her but never got the chance, because as soon as I answered, in a shattered voice that I had never heard from my wife before, Carol sobbed, "Peter, *it's cancer. It's cancer!*"

At first, I ridiculously thought she was playing a joke on me, just saying that to get back at me for my behavior earlier that day. But she would never be so cruel. What convinced me was her voice—I'll never forget that voice. It lacked all of the restraint that we normally subconsciously impose on our way of speaking. It was wild, hysterical, and unnerving, a voice a person never consciously uses but instead issues forth from some deep and terrible place, like when someone falls from a great height. It is the voice of terror, of mourning, of a broken heart. And with that voice, Carol told me the doctor had confirmed it was breast cancer, a particularly aggressive kind, and that she would need treatment right away.

It was as if a bomb went off at that moment, sucking all the air out of the room, the world becoming a silent, enormous vacuum. I, a pastor with great facility with words, who had preached endless sermons to endless numbers of people, could not find a single word for my own wife. But truly there was no trite word I could have thrown into that void to make Carol, or me, feel better. All I could bring myself to say in that moment was that she should come home as soon as possible.

But I know this for a fact: What would have made that one moment many times easier for my wife to bear was if she had not traveled to her doctor with the sense that her husband was upset at her for something that he himself had done wrong, but instead had received a sincere apology and a loving hug. I've learned since then that there are situations in life in which your response is not correctly measured by what you say after something has happened, but by what you said and did before. Because sometimes, something so terrible and shocking occurs that any words of comfort and encouragement you give in response will fall miserably short, and you must depend on the emotional cache you have accumulated before that point. And God help you if you have none. That was a hard lesson that I learned that day—that being a good husband means not just being there after bad news, but before as well.

An hour later, Carol came through the front door, and the face she wore broke my heart. Her eyes, usually so luminous and bright, were nothing more than pools of undiluted sadness, hidden under brows contorted with fear. Her tearstained cheeks were slack, as were her shoulders, both exhausted from crying. Filled with both shame and love, with leaden arms I reached out to her and finally gave her that hug that she had wanted earlier, but now, in a totally different context. Now I wasn't hugging her to apologize for playing video games too late into the night—I was hugging her to keep our world from falling apart. With tears streaming down both of our faces, we stood and clutched each other desperately, as we would for months afterward. To this day, I have never missed an opportunity to give my wife a hug. You never know what will happen to those you love when they walk out the door.

●　●　●

Carol and I didn't talk much in the days that followed her diagnosis, choosing instead to sit quietly for long periods and breaking the silence only to ask each other questions to which neither of us had anything close to an answer. "How are we going to tell the girls about this?" Carol asked me, her voice tinged with dread, and no wonder. Katie had just turned two the month before, and her older sister four only one day later. They were both still so young, nothing more than a little girl and a toddler. How could they process the news that their mother was sick? What would the word *cancer* mean to them? How could we prepare them for the changes that they would soon witness—the mastectomy, then chemotherapy? Would we also have to tell them about . . . death?

One afternoon we finally mustered up the courage to tell them the news. Carol started, "Sophia, Katie, come here." They came over to her like they always did, like little ducks taking shelter beneath her arms and nestling close. "Mommy . . . is very sick right now. I know she looks okay, but there's something in her body that is no good for her, and we have to get it out and make it go away. And the doctors are going to help us do that."

They looked up at her silently, not really understanding what she was saying, only knowing by the tone of her voice and by her tears that what she shared was grave.

I continued, "Mommy is going to go through a lot of changes soon, but she's going to be the same mommy, and she's going to be much better after all this. So you need to help Mommy and Daddy by being good girls and by praying every day that she will get better."

After a moment of silence, Sophia looked at me and asked, "What does she have, Daddy?"

For a second I hesitated, debating whether or not I should use that loaded word that always brings so much dread in its wake: *cancer*. But I decided that even if I didn't tell her exactly what it was, she would inevitably see its effects on her mother and on our lives—the doctor visits, the surgery, the physical and emotional burden Carol would endure. We might as well give her a word to attach to the reality that we now faced.

And so I answered her gently, "Cancer, Sophia. It's called breast cancer." I could tell by her expression that she had never heard that term before. But she would hear it many more times in the coming months. There was nothing more that we could share with them at that point, nothing that they could understand or would be all that helpful. All that was left for us to do was to hold hands together and pray, pray that God would heal Mommy and protect all of our family.

Next, I had to tell our church. At that time, our church met on the third floor of an august former embassy building in Columbia Heights. The room was surrounded by large windows, which gave us a full view of the bustling streets and sidewalks of the neighborhood and the old church buildings that sat on nearly every street corner. That Sunday twenty-five bright-eyed young adults sat in their seats, chatting cheerfully with one another and waiting to hear what God had planned next for our church.

Looking into their faces, I could hardly bring myself to break the news to them of Carol's diagnosis and the details that we had so far, which were few. After telling them what we knew, I also let them know that over the next few weeks, I would be consulting with mentors in the denomination to figure out if it was still a good idea to continue on with our church or if it was better to close it down.

They were speechless, their faces stricken. As young people, they had no idea how to react to this news, as it was so rare for someone in our age group to get cancer. But it was not only their youthfulness that made this news difficult to process. It was also the fact that Carol's diagnosis stood in such stark contrast to everything we had experienced up to that point. Our first few weeks and months as a church were filled with such remarkable promise, replete with what seemed like divine signs from God that this church was going to thrive. After those experiences, it was jarring for us to learn of Carol's diagnosis, like suddenly hitting a brick wall while doing seventy miles an hour on the highway. I knew that they were asking the same question I was, why God had allowed such a devastating thing to happen at such a promising point in our church's life. But that was a question that none of us could answer. As we did with Sophia and Katie, we closed our time by praying together, asking God for healing, comfort, and strength to endure the coming months.

I did a lot of praying on my own as well, more than I had ever prayed in my entire life. I prayed the first thing when I woke up. I would pray constantly throughout the day and before I slept. And the refrain for all those times was the same: "God, please heal Carol, please." I would wake up repeatedly in the middle of the night with one thought and prayer on my mind: "God, heal my wife," before drifting back off to sleep. Prayer was a place of solace, a place I could bring my burdens and troubles and find some measure of comfort.

But an unexpected and unwelcome emotion began encroaching into this refuge—betrayal. I began to feel betrayed by God. My prayers might begin, "God, again I ask you for healing for Carol and strength to persevere." But eventually, inevitably, deeper thoughts would follow: *But this wasn't supposed to happen, you know. This isn't right. Not to me and my family, not to Carol.* Because God knew I had been a good person, or tried to be. I had devoted my entire life to following and serving God, giving up a promising career in medicine to become a pastor. And I wasn't satisfied with just being in ministry but wanted to do great things for the sake of God, so I started up my own church. I was willing to live in a hard neighborhood, a place where my possessions and my family were often at risk. As a result, God was supposed to protect me and my family against the worst that the world had to offer.

But he didn't. He had broken his side of the promise and allowed my third child to be miscarried. He had permitted my house to get broken into, our home violated. He had let my wife get breast cancer, right as we were planting a church. This kind of thing wasn't supposed to happen to people who followed God. We were supposed to enjoy protection and blessing, not cancer. This was just so unfair. I felt betrayed by God because he had broken his promises.

Being a mature Christian and pastor, I tried my best to fend off this feeling. I reminded myself that I knew better and that there are no such promises in Scripture that a good life guarantees a lack of suffering. After all, Jesus obeyed his Father's will but was persecuted and suffered terribly. The disciples followed in the footsteps of their Lord, and experienced the same. It says it point-blank in 1 Peter 4:12: "Do not be surprised at the fiery ordeal that has come on you to test you, as though something strange were happening to you." God never promised us a life free from trial and hardship, and I knew that. I had learned that in seminary and had even preached that exact same message to others on many occasions.

And yet, despite the apostle Peter's words, despite all my good theology and good intentions, here I was, my prayer life infiltrated by the deep sense of betrayal I felt toward God. I realized then that although I had never consciously subscribed to the gospel of health and wealth—the ideology that following God ensured physical blessings—I must have subconsciously absorbed it. Some subtle form of it had worked itself into my heart and mind, and from countless sources. I had absorbed it from the pervasive culture of the American dream, which teaches us that everyone gets what they deserve. Those who work hard can expect a successful life. If you do not have a successful life, well, you have only yourself to blame. I inherited this mentality from my parents, who believed that their children's success would prevent them from suffering in the same way they had. This ideology had seeped into my mind through the media and through countless books, TV shows, and movies, where the good guy always gets the girl, and the bad guy his just deserts. Without my knowledge, and contrary to the Word, I had absorbed these beliefs to my very core.

But I had never before realized how deeply I subscribed to these ideas until Carol was diagnosed. It was as if that moment separated what I said I believed from what I truly did believe, and the gap between the two was larger than I had ever thought possible. That is one of the powerful effects of true suffering: It shakes you with such brute force that your true thoughts and true beliefs are laid bare, and anything to which you simply paid lip service goes flying by the wayside, unable to hold fast in the face of such turmoil.

Emotionally, I felt betrayed by God. But I was forced to confront the fact that he had never promised that we would never suffer, and it was hardly fair to keep God accountable to promises that he never made. God had not betrayed me, and neither had his Word. In truth, of all the influences in my life, it was God and his Word that had tried to prepare me for the possibility of suffering, or rather, the inevitability. What had betrayed me were my modern and privileged sensibilities, which were obsessed with keeping suffering at arm's length, and my diluted and selfish understanding of faith, which equated hard times with an absent or unloving God. It was they that had misled me and left me brutally unprepared for Carol's diagnosis, not God.

But God does make promises to us, although of a very different sort than we often imagine. This is what we are told in Isaiah 43:1–3:

> But now, this is what the Lord says—
>   he who created you, Jacob,
>   he who formed you, Israel:
> "Do not fear, for I have redeemed you;
>   I have summoned you by name; you are mine.
> When you pass through the waters,
>   I will be with you;
> and when you pass through the rivers,
>   they will not sweep over you.
> When you walk through the fire,
>   you will not be burned;
>   the flames will not set you ablaze."

There is a promise in this passage, but not the one that we think. It is not a promise that we will never suffer—in fact, the passage seems to imply that we will inevitably pass through river, water, and fire. But the promise that God makes is that when we do, *he will be with us*, and those waters will not overwhelm us, nor will the fire completely consume and set us ablaze. He does not promise that we will not suffer, but that when we do suffer, he will be there with us in the midst of it all. It is a promise, not of painlessness, but of his presence.

Psalm 23—that famous passage of comfort and encouragement—testifies to the same exact promise. In verse 4, it reads, "Even though I walk through the darkest valley, I will fear no evil, for you are with me; your rod and your staff, they comfort me." We often overlook this, but God does not promise that we will not see the valley of the worst, the valley of mourning and persecution and cancer, only that *when we do, he will be right*

81

there next to us. His rod and staff, which are the hallmarks of his presence, will comfort and encourage us.

God had never told me that we would never see this valley or walk this path. And in fact, the valley was only to get much darker in the coming weeks. He only promised that when I saw that terrible place, he would be there and would never abandon me. While I found real comfort in this, only time would tell whether he would be faithful to that promise or not.

5

A Drop in Coverage

Though the process of finding out about Carol's cancer had unfolded over the course of two months, Carol and I were still floored by the diagnosis. Nearly up to the last moment, we assumed everything would be fine, because breast cancer was one of those things that always happened to someone else, which is true, until the moment that "someone else" happens to be you. Upon hearing the news, we found ourselves in a state of utter shock.

So it was in many ways the best thing for us that after her diagnosis, Carol and I were funneled into the mammoth medical system set up for cancer patients, a predetermined course of appointments, tests, and conversations. Get this test, then talk to this doctor. Talk to that doctor, and then get this test. We felt like characters in a movie about communist Russia, going from line to line to get milk, then eggs, and then shuffling back to the milkman for butter, a gray-faced comrade punching our card at every stop. But we weren't complaining, far from it. Our health coverage was excellent, and our doctors both compassionate and professional. And when you have no idea what's going on, there is something immensely comforting about someone telling you what to do, where to go, and whom to talk to. It makes you think that someone out there knows what they're doing, even if you do not.

Added to this, the news we were getting from our initial doctor visits was encouraging. Some amazing advances in the treatment of breast cancer had been made in the past decade, advances that could treat the disease far more precisely, without harming healthy cells in the process. In fact, because of the development of targeted hormone therapies for breast cancer, many women were able to completely bypass chemotherapy altogether. The survival rates for breast cancer were good and climbing, with new medicines being researched and developed every year.

And so our shock gave way to a sense of guarded optimism. Yes, the whole breast cancer diagnosis had come out of nowhere. But we had health insurance and access to the best doctors and medical care. And breast cancer was treatable, with good survival rates. We began to feel hopeful, even confident, that we were going to beat this thing and move on with our lives. We smiled and laughed for the first time in weeks, expressions that were unthinkable for the first few days after the diagnosis. As long as nothing else went wrong from this point, we were going to make it.

After an especially grueling day of tests and doctor visits around the city, we came home both physically and emotionally exhausted. I sat down heavily in my favorite chair and stared blankly out of our front window, my favorite hobby ever since the diagnosis. It was November in D.C., and a few dried-up leaves clung tenaciously to the trees outside, as if denying that the onset of winter was imminent, clinging instead to the memory of warmer times. I sympathized.

Carol, being a more pragmatic person, opened the mail from the day. As I looked out the window, I could hear behind me the tearing of envelopes and crinkling of paper, but then, a peculiar kind of stillness as she read one letter in particular. Still vacantly staring out the window, I asked if anything was the matter and got no response. I turned in my chair to find her brow furrowed and face darkened as she pored over the letter she held in her hands. Alarmed, I rose from my chair and made my way over to her. I stood there for a minute more before she finally answered me.

"It's the insurance company. They're denying our coverage."

"What?!"

"They say my cancer was a preexisting condition. And since there was a gap in our health insurance coverage, they're not going to cover it."

"So what does that mean? That they're not going to pay for anything, none of the treatments at all?"

"I guess not."

I took the letter from her hands and read it for myself. After reading it a second and then third time, I closed my eyes as a crushing wave of despair washed over me. The fact that we had high-quality health insurance had been a crucial source of comfort for us, providing for us some semblance of peace of mind. But now even that was being ripped away from us at the worst possible moment. Carol could no longer just focus on beating the disease and getting better. We had to worry about how to pay for it all, whether she would be receiving the best care possible, and whether our family might be financially ruined as a result.

The growing confidence I had been feeling evaporated instantaneously, leaving in its wake a stark sense of abandonment and fear. How could this have happened? We had always been so careful with our health coverage. I had even turned down a pastoral position recently because the church would not offer full health care for my family and me. But somewhere along the way, we must have made some mistake, resulting in a break in coverage. I didn't know how we would move on from this point, how we could be expected to fight cancer without health insurance. Were you just supposed to show up at the emergency room and tell them to give you some chemo?

I was on the verge of surrendering to this terrible new development when Carol interrupted my thoughts with a simple question. "Wait. When did we ever have a gap in our health insurance?"

I took a moment to consider that. I had ended my tenure at my last church at the end of May of 2009 and began this church plant at the beginning of September in the same year—a period of exactly three months. My previous church had provided a small financial severance—I remembered that much. But I also recollected a conversation I had with the head pastor of that church before I left. He had personally called me into his office to inform me that the board of the church had decided to extend my health benefits for three months, just to make sure there were no problems when it came to coverage. I didn't think much of it at that time because I never dreamed it would be an issue of any kind. But this meant there had been no gap in health insurance coverage. After all, my previous employer had specifically continued our coverage for this specific reason. We immediately pored through our insurance records and verified that this was true. We had never been without health insurance, not even for a single day. That one simple act of generosity on behalf of our former church had saved us.

Carol immediately picked up the phone to call our health insurance provider. I assumed it wouldn't take long to clear this up, that they would quickly verify there had been no gap, apologize for the oversight, and reinstate our coverage. But as the minutes passed, I could tell by Carol's incredulous expression that this was not the case. Instead, the agent on the phone told her we would be required to send proof of coverage to them, or else their decision would stand. This made no sense to us whatsoever. Surely they already had all of this information on file in their immense database. It could not have been difficult for them to open our folder and verify that what we were telling them was the truth. But for some reason, they still wanted us to prove it.

I frantically motioned to Carol to hand the phone to me so that I might unleash the meaner side of my personality, the side that, as a pastor, I usually keep under wraps. But she waved me off, and instead of cursing the agent out, she politely said good-bye. She isn't that kind of person, the kind who gets mad. She prefers to get even. So with no small amount of malicious glee, she sent them, in triplicate, the records that verified that our coverage had always been continuous. This would settle the matter once and for all.

But it didn't, not for over a week. With each day that passed, I became more convinced they would stand by their refusal to cover Carol's treatments, and we would be on our own. Finally, after numerous phone calls to ask what was going on, we received a letter in the mail from our insurance company. In perfunctory and unapologetic language, they acknowledged that they had made a clerical oversight and agreed to continue to cover Carol's breast cancer treatments. Reading the letter together, we exhaled a huge sigh of relief. Thank God that we would not have to wage a battle on two fronts, simultaneously fighting cancer and our insurance company at the same time. Carol could just focus on getting better as soon as possible.

I was relieved, without a doubt. But I was also mad. Something about this situation did not sit right with me—the fact that they had denied us coverage even when it was crystal clear that our coverage was airtight. I was angry and curious, a dangerous combination. So I went on the Internet and searched for the terms *breast cancer, insurance,* and *cancellation.* What I discovered shocked and outraged me.

The federal government had brought a case against one of the largest health insurance companies in the United States. In it, they alleged that this company had used a mathematical algorithm to target people who had breast cancer or HIV, canceling their coverage on flimsy or even incorrect information or flagging them for aggressive fraud investigation. It was a practice known as "rescission," where insurance companies would use flimsy or even false pretexts to cancel the coverage of people whose treatments were especially expensive. The assumption was that most of these people would be too overwhelmed and intimidated to put up a fight and would instead simply acquiesce to the cancellation, which would save the company from having to pay for their costly treatments.[1]

Reading this report, I realized that's exactly what they had tried to do to us. When Carol was diagnosed, they must have flagged us for rescission, hoping that we would be too beleaguered to argue with their judgment, and they would be off the hook for her treatments. And I had almost fallen for it, until Carol had the presence of mind to question whether what they had determined was actually true. We were exceedingly lucky in that way. But I could

1. Murray Waas, "WellPoint routinely targets breast cancer patients," Reuters, April 23, 2010, http://www.reuters.com/article/2010/04/23/us-wellpoint-breast cancer-idUSTRE63M5D420100423.

easily imagine that many people who had just been diagnosed fell for this vile business practice, too overwhelmed by everything else they faced to question the decision of a giant company. Those people would be forced to pay for care in some other way and more than likely, would make compromises in the care they received. There would be delays in prognosis, delays in treatment, which would negatively affect outcomes. In other words, human beings probably died as a result of this business practice.

A week or so after this, I called the insurance company to ask them to mail me a document. The customer service agent was annoyingly cheery: "That's no problem, Mr. Chin. Now, what document do you want?"

"I want a copy of that letter you sent me informing me that my wife's treatments would not be covered."

She was silent for a moment before continuing: "Okay, Mr. Chin. Is there a reason you need that particular document?"

"I want a copy for my personal records."

Her merry tone noticeably slipped a few notches. It was now courteously wary. "I understand that, Mr. Chin. But we have to know if you're going to use that document for anything."

In a flash of insight, I knew why she was probing me on this. They were hesitant to provide me with that letter because they knew they had done something wrong and were afraid of the bad press. My anger made me eloquent, and mean.

"You want to know what I'm going to use it for? I'm going to frame it and hang it in my bathroom, right in front of my toilet. And that way, whenever I go in there, I can think of your company and what you tried to do to my wife. Why does it matter why I want it? You sent it to me; it's an official record, and I want it."

" . . . Okay. I'll forward that request to our records department. Is there anything else we can help you with today?" I knew this woman was not personally responsible for what had happened to us, but it didn't matter. My fury had overflowed its banks, and she was standing in its way.

"Yes, I have a question. You know that people die when you pull stunts like this, sending them unjustified letters of cancellation. You know that, right?"

"Mr. Chin . . ."

"Well, if you didn't, you do now. You can't claim ignorance. Have a great day, knowing that you work for a place that values money over human life."

"Okay, Mr. Chin . . . you have a good day too." I have to give her points for ending our conversation like that. But I never did receive that document, to this day.

● ● ●

If it's not abundantly clear, I was mad. Actually, "mad" is a pretty mild description of how I felt. It was closer to enraged, seething, wrathful. I was furious with our insurance company because they were supposed to be there if and when we got sick. Instead, they used that opportunity to hang us out to dry, with my wife's life on the line. That anger has barely subsided in the years since this took place.

But in the days following this debacle, I began to wonder if my anger was limited to the insurance company alone. Because in some way, hadn't God done the same thing to us? After all, Carol and I had always tried to play by God's rules and were careful and responsible in the living of our faith. And just like our insurance company, God was supposed to protect us and be there when we needed him. But when that moment came, it seemed he was nowhere to be found. At least the insurance company had the courtesy of sending us a letter informing us that they would be abandoning us.

These bleak thoughts simmered within me, and as they did, I could almost feel my faith wavering, like a house of cards with some terrible flaw at its base. I desperately tried to tamp down my anger and disappointment and hide them from everyone around me. There was no place where I felt I could share them safely. Carol was already dealing with enough, physically and emotionally, and did not need to hear me say things like that. Knowing my wife, she would just worry about me rather than focusing on herself and getting better, so I couldn't say anything to her, although she probably already knew how I felt.

I felt the same about my church. I could not let my congregation know the terrible thoughts that I now regularly entertained in my darkest moments. The church plant was only three months old at that point, just getting started in every possible way. How would it survive and flourish if their pastor was angry and mistrustful of God? It would be a death sentence to such a fledgling congregation.

In addition, I had always felt a tacit expectation from people that pastors were supposed to be stronger and more faithful than the average person—unflappable, if not bulletproof. And so I would put on a mask every Sunday. I would share how thankful we were for people's support and prayers, how we were already seeing God's providence and comfort, and how confident I was that God had a plan for everything we were experiencing, both personally and corporately. I was lying through my teeth, at least when it came to my supposed confidence in God's plan. In truth, the words that reflected my true thoughts and feelings would have shaken them deeply.

I hid these thoughts and feelings, not just to protect the ones I loved, but because I had always thought that God would never allow such terrible sentiments to be expressed. I had grown up in a number of different faith environments. I was born and baptized in the Roman Catholic Church, worked in a Pentecostal church, and then planted a church through the Evangelical Covenant Church, which was founded by Swedish Pietists.

But one of the most potent spiritual influences in my life was the Korean Presbyterian church where I was saved. I have a lot of respect for Reformed theology, of which Presbyterianism is a part. But by virtue of its structured and intellectually rigorous nature, it can sometimes lend itself to an extremely reverential view of God. In its more extreme forms, and in the hands of a clumsy person, Reformed theology can create a dogmatic and authoritarian conception of God that can be very difficult to relate to on a personal level.

When you marry this theology with Korean culture, which is already deeply hierarchical and respect-driven, it is a potent and often dangerous mix. As a result, some of my most formative years as a Christian were spent in a context in which God and his chosen leaders were never to be shown perceived disrespect of any kind. I still remember one of my very first Sundays at such a church. Intent on integrating my siblings and me into American culture, my parents never insisted that we speak Korean or learn Korean customs. All that mattered was straight As and an Ivy League degree. I knew only how to say my name in Korean and what the word for "idiot" was, because that is what my relatives would often derisively call me when they discovered how shoddy my Korean was. But beyond that, nothing.

In junior high, a friend of mine invited me to his Korean Presbyterian church, where I was given one of my first lessons on Korean culture. I was walking the hallways, completely lost, when a group of impressive older men passed me by. I watched them as they passed, but the youngest man of the group looked at me with an expression of hostile surprise. He walked right up to me and asked, "What are you doing?" Not knowing what the proper response to such a random question might be, I said nothing.

He continued, "Don't you know who this man is?" gesturing to the man who was at the front of the group. I said I had no idea. "He's the *mok-sah-neem*." I didn't have the slightest clue what that meant, although I would later learn it meant "ordained pastor" in Korean. He must have interpreted my clueless expression as a sign of calculated disrespect, because he went on: "Don't you think you should *in-sah* to the *mok-sah-neem*?" It was clear he wanted some response from me, so I ventured a timid "Yes?" I actually didn't know what *in-sah* meant but would learn it's the term for respectfully bowing to leaders or elders. But he seemed satisfied with this, and after flipping me another contemptuous look, he walked away with the head pastor, who I would later learn was his own father.

The lesson I learned that day was that clearly, one was never to be disrespectful, whether to God or his servants.

I had subconsciously internalized these principles. And so in those terrible days in November of 2009, I instinctively buried everything that I was thinking and feeling: the fear, the anger, the desolation. I hid them all away. I did this in order to protect my wife and children and to protect the young church I had planted. But I also did this out of respect for God, because I did not want to emotionally vomit upon a God who is so holy. To do so would have been wrong, and he was not worthy of such terrible and unholy thoughts.

Prayer became less of a refuge for me during that time than it had earlier, as it never failed to reveal the true state of my heart. I didn't appreciate having to stare into the abyss of my own soul on a daily basis. So I instead turned to Scripture, which seemed equally godly but a little less personally revealing, a good compromise from my point of view. And I was surprised to discover that Scripture was full of emotional vomit.

There are numerous moments in the Bible where people cry out to God in desperate and even theologically suspect complaint. An entire book of the Bible is called "Lamentations." And many of the psalms are filled with complaint, and although many of these end with celebration of God and his good works, some do not. Most notoriously, there is a terrible verse at the end of Psalm 137, where the psalmist concludes with this: "Happy is the one who repays you according to what you have done to us. Happy is the one who seizes your infants and dashes them against the rocks" (vv. 8–9).

Ugh.

What an awful thing to say, a perfect example of an ignominious sentiment that hardly squares with the compassion and love of God. I don't think in any way that God celebrates something so utterly reprehensible as the violent murder of infants. So why is it in Scripture then?

It's placed in Scripture, not as a prescription of sorts, as if to tell us that we are supposed to *do* such a thing. Rather, it's in there because it tells us that we are allowed to *say* such a thing. God allows us to express ourselves, even in ways that are immature and unrefined or even straight-up wrong, not because such thoughts are right or justified, but because he loves us enough to allow them and is gracious enough to absorb them without striking us down.

Lament can be hard for us to accept, much less practice, especially for those who come from strict theological and cultural traditions similar to my own. But Christ himself gave voice to his anguish while hanging on the cross. With his hands outstretched and pierced, a crown of thorns jammed tightly on his head, he cried out in Aramaic, *"Eloi, Eloi, lama sabachthani?"* which translates to "My God, my God, why have you forsaken me?"

There is a convincing theological explanation for this moment, that Jesus' cry was a reflection of the fact that the whole of human sin had been placed on his body, and so for the first time in all of history, he was truly separated from the holy presence of God the Father, with whom he had shared communion since the beginning of time. So Jesus' lament was not theologically incorrect, not in the same way that many of our own laments tend to be.

But I think that to some small degree, Jesus said this simply because this was how he felt in that moment—abandoned, forsaken, and alone, and one can hardly blame him. Even though Jesus knew that his Father had not forsaken him, and that his crucifixion was not truly abandonment in an eternal sense but part of a greater plan to redeem a broken creation, Jesus felt forsaken and abandoned and was permitted to express that pain. And if Jesus was allowed to do so, perhaps we are allowed to do the same.

Now, I should make clear that we can go too far with this principle and share our thoughts and feelings in a way that is closer to crass complaint than true lament, or in a manner that lacks grace and self-control and can destroy the faith of others. I am not condoning either of these. Neither should we ever simply throw good theology out the window for the sake of "being honest," nor should we ever forget that God is holy, even terrifyingly so.

And yet, neither should we forget that to the degree that God is holy, he is equally loving. He is a holy judge, but as we read in 1 Peter 3, he is eternally patient and wants none to perish. He is the King who had no sin, but who went to the cross to bear ours. He is a God who by all rights could strike us down but instead chose to be struck and to see us as his children, prodigal and precious in equal measure. This is the mystery of the character of God, and as confounding as it might be, we must live in light of both of these truths, not simply one or the other. As controversial as it might sound, I think during the worst moments of our lives, we can be honest with God, even if our honesty is a little raw, negative, and even incorrect. God is big enough to take it.

I pondered this idea for a long while. Then, taking a deep breath and trying to ignore a decade's worth of experiences in the Korean church, I began to pray in a way I never had:

"God, why did you abandon us? I was trying to do your work and follow your will. It's not like I expected things to be perfect, but I expected some kind of blessing and protection and favor, or at the very least, that Carol would not get breast cancer. What kind of God allows this to happen to people who try their best for him?

"And now what? What will you allow next? Because if you allowed Carol to get sick and for our insurance to get canceled, will you let Carol die, for me to be left without my wife, my daughters without their mother? Would you take my life, leaving my children with no parents? Are there any limits to what you won't allow? How am I supposed to trust you?!"

I carried on like this for quite a while, but at some point, I finally slowed down and stopped, my frustrations spent. To be honest, it didn't feel good to say these things, not in the way it feels good to vent at people you feel have done you wrong. These thoughts and complaints brought me no pleasure to consider or to voice. But it felt good in the sense that it was a reminder of how large and loving God is—that I could say these things and not be struck down, that his love for me would be constant. And this might have been the best thing for me at the time. Because I was going to have to be absolutely certain of God's love for me in order to prepare for what we were going to learn next.

Triple Negative

That winter Carol and I spent a lot of time in waiting rooms, which is a universally unpleasant experience. But to make things worse, these were oncology waiting rooms, which make for a unique sort of unpleasant experience. They invariably featured muted lighting and an artificial waterfall of some kind, recycled water being poured over rocks, designed to inspire a peaceful and meditative state of mind for cancer patients. To me, they were an insult to meditative gardens everywhere. I wondered what edition of *SkyMall* they had been ordered from and looked for a button in the back of the piece to press in order to hear a whale song.

What made these visits even worse for us was the fact that we felt so out of place. Because we were going to see breast cancer specialists, the other patients sitting next to us were usually older women, in their fifties and sixties and older. There were never any young women present. These older patients were not mean to us in any way, but the exact opposite, regarding us with deep compassion and pity. While well intentioned, this made us feel absolutely wretched. If an old and gaunt cancer patient is looking at you with pity in her eyes, you know you're in deep trouble. Even among these people with whom we shared so much in common, we felt isolated and alone.

But at least we had each other. My conscience still stung from my complete failure as a husband when Carol was first diagnosed. So I resolved to accompany Carol to every appointment I possibly could so that she would never have to face bad news alone again. Fortunately, my schedule as a pastor was flexible enough to make this feasible. In December of 2009, we found ourselves at the office of Carol's breast cancer surgeon, Dr. Griffin. She would be performing Carol's mastectomy and was about to explain more of the details about Carol's cancer.

I liked Dr. Griffin a lot. She was a surgeon with decades of expertise. She also struck Carol and me as very confident and yet very caring, a good combination for a doctor and a particularly rare one in surgeons, who tend to be more of the former and less of the latter. But there was also this very likable air about her, a kind of rough-hewn and sardonic humor that I assume came from raising three teenage sons. I think women in that situation, as a survival mechanism, develop a sarcastic view of life and a high tolerance for potty humor and jokes involving the butt and/or farts. She also respectfully referred to me as "Reverend," which I thought was rather nice of her, considering I look like a teenager.

We were sitting in her office as Dr. Griffin explained the details of Carol's pathology report from her biopsy. We had tried to read it over ourselves, and despite our backgrounds in science, we were completely bewildered by the technical medical language. Medical vocabulary seems to possess a mysteriously misleading quality to it, where one can't be sure if the term *positive* means something truly positive at all. She started off by explaining to us that Carol's cancer was stage 2, meaning that the tumor was around two centimeters long.

Carol said, "So that's good, right, because cancer staging goes up to 4. So we caught it pretty early?"

"Yes, you did. At stage 2, it's very treatable, and the prognosis is quite good," she responded. I relaxed my shoulders.

"But . . ." she continued, my shoulders tensing right back up, "I did a manual examination of your lymph nodes in your armpit, and I'm fairly certain the cancer has already spread there. So more precisely, we would call this stage 2b. Because of this, it's important that we get the tumor out as soon as possible."

The news that the tumor had started to spread made me apprehensive, so I began to probe for some good news in all of this.

"How about after the surgery, the chemotherapy treatments? I've been reading that some women don't even have to do chemotherapy because they can take hormone therapy as well. Is that possible for us?"

At this, Dr. Griffin took a deliberate and lengthy pause, which I instinctively knew was not a good sign. "Unfortunately, no. Your tumor is negative for any hormone receptors, which means we can't use hormone therapy to stop its growth. We'll have to go with more standard treatments, which include surgery, chemotherapy, and radiation."

Carol and I shot a glance at one another. This was a major blow. One of the reasons we had started to feel hopeful was the prospect that Carol might avoid chemotherapy and take advantage of the amazing new treatment options that had been recently developed. But now we were being told those treatments would be useless for us. We would have to rely on chemotherapy, a powerful but heavy-handed option where chemicals would be pumped through Carol's entire body, killing any cell that dares divide more rapidly than it should, including cancer cells . . . hair, fingernails, red blood cells, eggs. It is an effective treatment, but not a very specific one, since it affects a person's entire body, not just the cancer itself. It's kind of like trying to shoot a duck with a flamethrower.

I swallowed hard and tried not to let the despair show on my face as I looked at my wife. Her face was impassive, and I wondered if she was thinking the same thing.

Dr. Griffin was careful in her next statement. "Carol, your cancer is a very specific type. It's called triple negative, because it's negative for any of those hormone receptors." She took another pause and then with renewed enthusiasm said, "But we still are going to treat it; we're going to take the tumor out of you during surgery, and then chemotherapy will take care of any remaining cancer cells, and radiation will make sure it doesn't come back." She said this with real conviction and confidence, which was heartening. But at the same time, I could tell by her tone of voice and the deliberateness with which she spoke that there was more to this "triple negative" designation. What did that really mean?

"What about the mastectomy?" Carol asked. "Will I be getting a lumpectomy or a full mastectomy?" With a lumpectomy, just the tumor is removed and most of the breast spared, while in a mastectomy, the entire breast is surgically removed. Shaking her head, Dr. Griffin explained: "Again, because your tumor is triple negative, we have to be really aggressive in treating it. I think we have to do a mastectomy, just to make sure we remove it all." I sank even lower in my chair. Was there any good news in any of this?

She went on: "But even with a mastectomy, you do have the option to have reconstructive plastic surgery, so it wouldn't look different from before. Is that something you want to do?" Carol immediately shook her head. Doing a reconstruction would just mean more surgery and an even longer recovery time, neither of which she was interested in. But this was only part of her reasoning. In a conversation with her later, she told me how in Afghanistan she had seen amputees who were the victims of mines and had marveled at their lack of self-consciousness. They never allowed the loss of a limb to affect their self-worth. She decided not to get reconstruction because she did not want to be defined by one part of her body, or the absence thereof. If they could live without an arm or both legs, then she could live without her breast. As she told me this, I stared at her in amazement. Evidently, I had married Wonder Woman.

We left our meeting with Dr. Griffin with ambivalent feelings, encouraged by the confidence and experience of our surgeon and by the fact that surgery was imminent, but apprehensive about what we had discovered about the tumor itself—that it would not respond to modern therapies and was so aggressive that nothing short of a full mastectomy would be considered adequate. And again, the question struck me—what was "triple negative"?

I was determined to find out more about Carol's type of cancer and had an idea of how I might learn more. Since Carol had to take care of a few administrative matters in another part of the hospital, I told her I had a phone call to make and would catch up with her there. But instead, I headed back to the oncology department and struck up a conversation with a doctor who was in the hallway. This was not something I was prone to doing, but I was on a mission. I just had to find out more.

I wanted to hear the unvarnished truth about this type of cancer, so I didn't tell the oncologist that my wife had been diagnosed. Instead, I casually asked her, "I've heard about something called triple negative breast cancer. What is that?"

Perhaps thinking I was just a high school student who was interested in the subject, she launched into an enthusiastic summary. "Researchers are discovering that there isn't just one type of breast cancer, but different types. Each type is identified by hormone markers on the surface of the tumor—some have estrogen receptors and are called estrogen positive, and so on. The term 'triple negative' means that there are no hormone receptors there, which is a problem because a lot of treatments shrink tumors by binding with those hormone receptors." I nodded. So far, this lined up with what we had been told by Dr. Griffin. But the doctor was not finished yet.

"But beyond this, triple negative is just about the worst kind of breast cancer you can get. Not only is it harder to treat, it's really aggressive, and it likes to spread. The tumors exhibit low differentiation, meaning they are loose and metastasize quickly. And worse of all, TNBC comes back frequently—a high rate of recurrence. For some reason, it is especially prevalent in young women. In fact, a lot of breast cancer specialists call it a killer of young women."

My blood froze in my veins. *A killer of young women . . .* like my wife?

I abruptly made some excuse to the doctor and then turned and walked away quickly. She must have thought I was a lunatic. Little did she know that she had just informed me that not only did my wife have breast cancer, but she had the worst type of breast cancer possible.

For the next few days, I began to desperately hunt for more information, for any positive sign or encouragement that we could latch on to. I devoured information on every legitimate website I could find, any resource that could give me some reason to be hopeful. But the news regarding triple negative breast cancer was uniformly bleak. Night after night, I would read and re-read the horrible details in disbelief. Triple negative was characterized by its resistance to treatment. High recurrence. High rates of metastasis. And high rates of mortality. I would read unblinking, the bright screen searing those words into my vision so I could see them even when I closed my eyes: *recurrence, metastasis, mortality.*

One night, as Carol and I lay in bed, I turned over to face her and said, "Carol? I want you to promise me something."

"What is it, honey?"

"Promise me that you won't look up anything on triple negative."

She waited a moment before responding. "Why?"

"Just promise me—I think it would be better for you."

For most people, this would be nothing more than an invitation to begin researching it right away. But my wife is a person of simple faith and trust, so she responded, "Okay. I promise." And I knew that she wouldn't. I'm sure that some people might disagree with my request, believing it is better to be completely cognizant of what you face so as not to be under any illusions. I can see the logic of that. But I asked her to do this in order to preserve that incredibly precious and limited resource: hope. I thought that if she knew what triple negative was really like, all hope would be lost, and so would we.

Fear began to grip me in a way I had never experienced before. It was constant, refusing to abate, even while I was sleeping. I scarcely slept and, when I did, was plagued by dreams and half-remembered visions of loss and sorrow. I would wake up from these dreams with a start, trying to discern what was real and what was imaginary, and would despair when I realized that our waking reality was only slightly better than the nightmare. Eventually, after days of this, something deep inside me broke. The initial cancer diagnosis itself had been bad enough,

103

especially because it was so shocking and unexpected. But we had bravely soldiered on and kept the faith. And then to have our insurance taken away, even briefly, we were brought to our knees emotionally, unsure what we knew about God and how he worked. But then to discover that not only did Carol have cancer, but a particularly deadly type—triple negative—I was brought from my knees all the way to the floor, nose shoved into the dirt. I realized that everything I had learned about God and his ways, whether implicitly or explicitly, was questionable. I knew nothing about him.

I had always assumed that I could call God my Shield, my Protector, my Healer, as countless words from Scripture and sermon and worship songs had always asserted. But I experienced none of those things in my own life, just wave after wave of the most bitter discouragement. How could a God who allowed this to happen to my wife and best friend be trusted, or considered loving, in any way? Perhaps the God I was seeing now was the one who God truly was—cold, untrustworthy, frightening. My conception of God—built on years of being a Christian, attending and serving at church, and even studying the Bible at a graduate level—came crashing down upon me, a glass house shattered in a hailstorm of suffering and discouragement.

I had finally hit bottom.

●　●　●

I had a recurring dream during that time. In it, Carol would be lying on a hospital bed or gurney, and I would be sitting next to her. She was motionless, and it was never quite clear if she was just sleeping, or something worse. Sophia and Katie would walk into the room and see their mother lying there and begin to weep, tears streaming down the sides of their cheeks, their little faces contorted with grief. It was then I knew that Carol was not asleep. She was dead. I would always wake up at that moment with a gasp and turn quickly in my bed to check on Carol. She was lying there, still but breathing, sleeping peacefully.

About the fourth or fifth time I had this dream or some nightmarish variation of it, I turned to make sure that Carol was all right, and afterward began to weep, not in relief but in exhaustion. I couldn't take it anymore—the fear, the uncertainty, the thought of losing my wife. Not wanting to wake Carol, I left our bed, went into the bathroom, and closed the door. But when my sobbing refused to subside, I went downstairs to the living room instead. Even that wasn't enough. Eventually my crying became so deep and uncontrollable that I had to go down into the basement so I could give voice to my trauma without traumatizing those I loved, a three-story kind of weeping.

But as I wept and mourned in the pitch-blackness of my basement, something inside of me, a voice or a presence, maybe both, suddenly said,

"STOP CRYING."

"STOP COMPLAINING."

"THIS IS REAL LIFE, AND THIS IS YOUR LIFE. SO STAND UP AND BE STRONG. YOU REALLY DON'T HAVE ANY OTHER CHOICE."

I can't say for certain it was the voice of God. But these words did issue from some deep place within me. And they shocked me to the core. If this message was from God, it was not the encouragement I had been expecting. I always imagined that if there was to be a great emotional or spiritual epiphany in that season, it would come from being reminded of God's love and faithfulness, something softer and more sympathetic.

But what these words lacked in gentleness, they made up in raw truth. Thousands of women had breast cancer. Millions more had cancer of other types. In fact, many children had cancer, and I had seen them at the hospital receiving treatment, precious children with wonderful smiles and no hair, dark circles under their eyes. I knew that some of them would not survive their trial and never have the chance to live half the life that my wife and I had already enjoyed. Countless others had ailments that were equally terrible and life threatening, or more so. In the midst of everything we were going through, I had never realized our situation was not extraordinary. This was real life for so many, and now, for us. And my previous perspective— that tenacious assumption that our situation was unique in some way—was a lie, an illusion fostered by a sheltered and comfortable existence.

Moreover, crying and complaining would do us no good right now. They would not change our situation or magically make Carol better. In fact, they would do the opposite, only frightening the rest of my family, as well as weakening my own resolve by keeping my own eyes stubbornly focused on how I felt and not on what I needed to do. I had no choice but to play the cards I had been dealt instead of lamenting the fact that I had not been given the cards I wanted.

Such thoughts might seem like a contradiction to what I shared earlier, how there is a place for complaint in the Christian life because the love of God is vast enough to absorb such sentiments. I still stand by that belief. But I recognize that even though there is a time for complaint, there is also a time for complaint to cease. Introspective lament may have its place, in Scripture and in our lives. But it also should have an end point, at which point we should be prepared to dust ourselves off and face the reality that is before us. And nowhere do we see this more clearly than in the life of Christ himself, in the garden of Gethsemane.

There, Jesus was faced with a terrible fate: his imminent arrest at the hands of the authorities who would whip him and beat him and then nail him to a cross, where he would hang for hours. The Gospel of Matthew describes Jesus' thoughts in detail, calling him anguished and distressed, or in his own words: "My soul is crushed with grief to the point of death." He cried out to God, using a term of intimate endearment: "Abba! Daddy, save me! But not my will—yours." He would say that two more times, swollen drops of sweat falling to the ground like blood.

But the prayers did not go on like that forever. After the third prayer, Jesus arose and told his disciples to get up as well. "The time has come," he said, "for the Son of Man to be betrayed into the hands of sinners." And then, he courageously walked directly to his fate. Jesus lamented, it's true. But when it was time to get up, *he got up.*

And so I did the same. I stopped crying and wiped my tears. And as I did, it was like a veil had been torn from my eyes, like I was seeing life clearly for once. Yes, our situation was a difficult one, a terrible one. That was the truth. But it was also a terribly common situation. And piteous crying and complaining would not change that fact. Perhaps they had had their time and place, but now it was time for such things to stop. This was the moment at which I needed to stand up and be strong, for my wife, for my daughters, and for my church. This was a moment made for faith.

This is not to say that I had never used my faith before then, but it was mostly to help me face the piddling everyday inconveniences of modern life: "God, help me deal with annoying co-workers. God, help me discern which of these two awesome jobs is your eternal will. God, help me to not blurt out curse words while driving. In Jesus' powerful name, amen." But this is not what faith is for—not really. Faith is not a breathing exercise

107

to make us feel marginally more at peace in the midst of modern distraction. It is stern stuff that allows a person to stare into the darkest void and walk straight in. Faith was made for hardship, suffering, fear, and sickness, for nights like that night.

The following night was very different from the previous one. Out of habit, I continued to search for information on triple negative breast cancer, even though I already knew every statistic out there. But as I read these articles again, my response was different. I didn't find them nearly as frightening, and to be honest, they didn't cause much of an emotional response at all. All I thought was, *Okay. This doesn't change anything, really.* Whether it was triple negative or not, good prognosis or bad, nothing was changed about the next nine months of our lives. Carol would have to get surgery, chemotherapy, and then radiation. After that, we would wait and pray, but most important, we would live our lives as we had before. That was all we could do, all we could control, and everything else was in God's hands. Now considering what my conception of God was at that time, "God's hands" were not all that comforting of an image. But still, it was better than drowning in fear. The terror that had gripped me was gone, replaced with resolve and sober-mindedness.

It may seem prosaic to say it, but I consider this the moment I became a man. I don't say that in some testosterone-fueled attempt to reclaim masculine Christianity. I'm of the opinion that Christianity is more of a divine thing than a masculine one. Plus, the strongest person I know in the world is a woman, so I hardly believe that internal fortitude is encoded on the Y chromosome alone. But the moment I became a man wasn't when I got married, nor was it when we had our first child or our second. Any idiot can do that, and many idiots do. No, I counted myself a man when I realized that life was hard and unfair, but that faith was made for "hard" and "unfair." Faith shows its true power and full worth in such moments.

● ● ●

I have to admit this revelation went to my head a bit. In addition to feeling less fearful, I started to strut around the house a lot more, confident in my newfound Christian manliness. Carol even began to notice a change in my facial expressions. In the first few weeks after the diagnosis, I had the dazed look of a deer in the headlights or maybe even a dog who had been abused and startled at every motion and raised hand. But at some point, Carol told me, my face changed. My eyes squinted and eyebrows furrowed, as if I were going for the world record for the longest Clint Eastwood impersonation. I had no idea that I was doing that and told her so. She asked if I was worried about something, and I laughed grimly.

"Of course I'm worried about something!"

"No, no," she replied. "Worried about something more!"

"You mean more than you having cancer? And trying to plant a brand-new church at the same time?"

"Yes," she said with a sigh, rolling her eyes at my heavy-handed attempt at sarcasm.

I dramatically took a deep breath and related my experience in the basement. I told her how I felt like God was telling me to stop crying, put fear aside, and focus more on taking care of what was in front of us. Perhaps that's why my face looked grim and Clint Eastwoody—it was a reflection of this new conviction. I looked at her expectantly, thinking she would fawn over my manly courage.

"That's actually what I do every day," she said.

I swear, at that moment I heard a sound, "*PSSSSSSSSsssss* . . ." like the sound of a balloon losing air, or in this case, my ego shrinking to its more normal and deflated size. Crestfallen, I asked her what she meant, and she explained: "I feel frightened about the cancer and what's going to happen, but I try to let myself feel it only for a limited time. After a while, I push it aside and take care of whatever I have in front of me."

I realized then that this is why my wife was able to face her diagnosis with such composure. It wasn't because she didn't feel the fear and anxiety, or that she didn't understand the nature of triple negative breast cancer. It was not my clumsy request that she not look up anything on triple negative that protected her from losing hope. It was because she gave that fear only a certain amount of space and time in her life, after which she would push it to the margins and get busy with living. Her courage was not a personality trait, but a conscious choice that she made every morning and several times a day.

I realized something else in that moment as well: that every night, I slept next to the bravest person I had ever met. Triple negative cancer was frightening, to be sure. But it had nothing on my wife.

"He's Up to Something"

By early January of 2010, we were getting ready to start the first step of Carol's treatment: a mastectomy to remove her right breast and some of the lymph nodes in her right arm. Those dry clinical terms mask the reality of what a mastectomy truly is—an amputation. And as with any amputation, mastectomies are followed by a recovery that is not only physical, but also emotional in nature. This is especially true in the case of mastectomies, as women lose a part of their body that is not just practical in function, but is intimately connected to their view of self and beauty. But in the inverted nature of life after cancer, we were relieved and even excited at the prospect that someone was going to amputate part of her body, because this meant the tumor was finally going to be removed as well.

You know you're in a strange and unfamiliar place when an amputation elicits feelings of relief and excitement.

Although the more debilitating sense of fear I had been experiencing had mostly been dispelled at this point, what had taken its place was an equally acute sense of cynicism. The past six months of our lives had taught me to always expect the worst. First it was the miscarriage, then the break-in at the house. Following that was Carol's diagnosis, the temporary loss of our health insurance, and the dire details about triple negative. As a result, I was ever anticipating another piece of bad news, another kick to the teeth. You could never let your guard down, and you could never assume that life could not get a little worse than it already was. The moment you did, life would take that opportunity to show you something new and terrible to make you scream in terror and frustration. This is how I felt about life, and things were no different the day Carol went in for surgery.

A good friend of ours came over that morning to babysit our daughters, and Carol and I left for Sibley Hospital. Sibley is a nice facility, located on the far western edge of the city, north of the cobblestone streets of Georgetown and south of Bethesda, home to a luxury shopping district that features quaint mom-and-pop stores like Cartier, Tiffany, and Bulgari. To be honest, I have no idea what they sell in any of those stores, just that whatever it is, I can't afford it. Because of the hospital's distance from our house, and the paralyzing morning traffic in the city, I was afraid we might be late. More than that, part of me was counting on some bizarre happenstance to bar our way to the hospital. After all, it's what I had come to expect out of life. But somehow we managed to get through the city without a single incident and arrived at the hospital exactly when she was scheduled to check in: 9:00. I marveled at our luck.

As we got into the hospital elevator, I would not have been entirely surprised if the cable had snapped and we were sent hurtling into the hospital basement. And while groaning amidst that smoking wreckage, our insurance company would have immediately called my phone to inform me that this would not be covered, as it was a preexisting elevator condition. But the elevator doors did open, and we were now only twenty short yards away from the front desk of the surgery ward. The end was in sight—we were going to make it.

We approached the front desk, and with a comforting sort of smile, the nurse on duty told us we were right on time. I think she said that for my benefit, as something in my face clearly communicated a need for reassurance. All she needed was some form of identification from Carol, and then she would be admitted for surgery. I finally allowed myself to breathe a sigh of relief. I may have even smiled at that point, although it had been a while since I had done so.

As I indulged myself in a thin and awkward grin, Carol rummaged in her purse for her driver's license. But after a few minutes of searching, I realized that something was wrong.

"Honey," she whispered, "I left my driver's license at home. On the dining table. I knew you would be driving, and I just . . . I just assumed I wouldn't need it."

My grin ran screaming for the hills. *I knew it.* I knew we could not go one entire morning without something terrible happening to us, for such had become our lot in life. And God forgive me for this, but I was annoyed at my wife. Never mind the fact that forgetting important things at home was definitely more of my calling card than hers—I was exasperated with her. Still, seeing the pained expression on her face, I summoned up my patented brave smile and proceeded to lie through my teeth.

"It'll be okay. Don't worry—I'm sure everything will be fine. Hmm. Let me call some people and see if they can get it from the house."

The nurse looked between my wife and me and apologized for the inconvenience. "I'm sorry about all this. It's just that

113

we need to verify your identity before we get started. I'll let the surgeon and the team know about the delay, and hopefully, they can wait until you can go and get it."

"Hopefully?! What does that mean?" I squeaked.

"Well, if it takes too long, they may just opt to cancel the surgery for today and reschedule for a later time."

It was at that moment that I truly and completely forgot how to smile.

In my fragile state, without an emotional floor beneath my feet, this minor inconvenience was nothing less than a catastrophe. Rescheduling was not an option, because all that would do is give the cancer a few more days or even weeks to divide and further spread to another part of Carol's body. This might seem like the ravings of a pathological cynic, but given the frightening details I had learned about triple negative breast cancer, it was not unjustified. My mind raced as I considered our options: Our babysitter could not drive over with the license because she didn't have car seats for our daughters. If I tried to go back to get it, it would take me over an hour, and the surgery would probably be canceled.

My only choice was to ask someone who lived near us to go and pick up the license and then drive it clear across the city. But to further complicate even this option, we had just moved to D.C. only a few months before and knew very few people who lived near us. In utter desperation, I called the one and only person who I knew worked close to my home: my mechanic, Steve. That's how desperate I was. Now, to be fair, he was also a friend of mine, but still, getting him to do us this favor was a long shot at best. As I punched in his number, I again prepared myself for disappointment.

In a strained and harried voice, Steve answered, "Hello, who's this?" See? A mechanic to his core.

"Hey, Steve, it's Pastor Peter Chin."

In an only slightly more congenial tone: "Oh. Hey."

"Steve, I'm in a real jam. Carol is going into surgery right now, but she forgot her license at home, and she needs it to get admitted. Would you . . . would you be able to go to our house and pick it up and then bring it to Sibley? There's someone there looking after the girls; you would just have to pick it up from her. But I know it's a long way, and—"

Before I could say any more, Steve cut me off with his usual brusqueness. "Yeah, no problem—where do you live?"

I gave him the address of our home and the hospital, and in thirty-three minutes, Steve managed to get to my house, pick up my wife's license from our babysitter, and make his way across the city during rush hour traffic. When he pulled into the hospital parking lot, I was waiting for his car and grabbed the license from him, but not before giving him my heartfelt and breathless thanks.

In typical Steve-the-mechanic-and-awesome-friend fashion, he dryly replied, "Sure. Good luck."

I then sprinted back inside the hospital and forced and bullied my way into an already overcrowded elevator. I remember my elevator mates looking at me not with annoyance, but with compassion, figuring that if I was running that fast in a hospital, there was probably a very good reason for it. A hospital may be the only place left in America where people still extend such sympathy to one another.

As I ran up to the front desk and slammed that piece of plastic in front of the nurse, she looked at me with wide eyes of surprise. I think she was shocked that I had gotten it so fast, but also that I had taken her words about rescheduling with such absolute gravity. And sensing my urgency, she hurried to get Carol checked in. After a few anxious minutes, she told us the surgery would still go ahead as planned and without delay. And for the first time in thirty-three minutes, I exhaled. We had made it. But frankly, my heart could not take another surprise today.

●　●　●

I sat in the waiting room, waiting for Carol's surgery to start. The nurse said she would come and get me so I could talk to Carol before they wheeled her in. Earlier I said that oncology waiting rooms are the worst, but that isn't true. Surgery waiting rooms alone hold that title. They seem ordinary enough, a squarish room lined with uncomfortable chairs, TVs bolted to the walls, always set on mute and to a channel that you would never choose to watch, if given the choice: the Weather Channel, CNBC, the Home Shopping Network.

But that's what I find so bizarre and jarring. These rooms are identical to any other waiting room you find in modern life, giving you the mistaken sense that you are waiting for something entirely mundane to take place, like for the bus or the lady at the DMV to finally call your number. The reality is, you are waiting for a doctor to use a knife to tear into the body of a person you care about, fool around in there for a while, and then sew that person back up, hoping everything will be better than it was before. While sitting in that room, life and death hang in the balance. It would be far more appropriate to install chapels outside of surgical wards instead of waiting rooms and replace all those uncomfortable chairs with kneelers, equally uncomfortable but far more appropriate, given the circumstances.

I had been waiting for half an hour already, but no one had come to tell me that Carol's surgery was about to get started. It wasn't supposed to take this long. For some reason, the mastectomy had been delayed. I knew it then: Something was wrong.

I steadfastly kept my eyes on the TV and flipped through a magazine or two, but it was no use. A palpable sense of dread fell on me, and my heart began to race—I knew something was not right.

That's when I felt a tap on my shoulder. It was Dr. Griffin.

"Reverend, I need to talk to both you and your wife about something very important. Will you come with me into surgical?"

Although I didn't say a word in response, my mind silently screamed in terror. I followed her through the automated double doors that led to the surgical prep room. With every step came rising dread that I could barely stifle. *What is it this time? The insurance company? Has the cancer spread to her lungs, to her brain? Is there some other terrible complication that we never could have imagined? What terrible news does God have in store for us?*

I followed Dr. Griffin into the surgery prep room, where my wife lay on a surgical gurney. My wife is not a large person at all, but lying on a hulking gurney and draped in her billowing surgical gown, she looked more like a child than the mother of two children. It broke my heart to see her this way, so fragile and so small. I reached out my hand to comfort her, to lend her any strength I could, but the truth was that I had none to give. I was terrified of what the surgeon would say next and could barely remain standing myself.

Dr. Griffin paused for a moment and regarded us with an inscrutable expression on her face, a mixture of both seriousness and, strangely, amusement. She began cautiously.

"Sooo . . . we took a routine blood test for your wife as we were prepping her for surgery, something we always do. But when I got the results back, I saw that her hormone levels were a little strange, a little unexpected. So we had to run some additional tests, which is why we haven't gotten started with the surgery yet." She paused again, whether to collect herself or for effect, I'll never know.

She plunged on. "I just got those results back right now. I took one look at them, and said to myself, 'OH . . . MY . . . GOD.' Mr. and Mrs. Chin: You are pregnant."

Carol and I looked at each other but didn't say a thing. Not a word. I think I tried to smile weakly at her, but I'm sure it was more of a frozen look of astonishment than anything else. A series of rather asinine questions raced through my mind: *Pregnant? How did she get pregnant? Can someone with cancer even get pregnant? And when did that happen, four weeks ago? That was during that huge snowstorm where we were stuck at home for the whole week, with nowhere to go. . . .*

Okay, I guess that makes sense.

Realizing we didn't have anything intelligible to say in response, Dr. Griffin continued, "Now, at this point we have to make some important decisions. First off, you are going to have this baby, right?"

You are going to have this baby, right?

It really wasn't just a question, because it was far more leading than that—it was more of an assumption, a suggestion even. The curious phrasing of her question sparked something in us, a conviction that we might not have had otherwise. Carol and I looked at each other for just the briefest of moments and immediately agreed: "Yes, of course. Of course we are going to keep this baby."

And that became our final decision—that no matter what happened, *we were going to keep this baby*. It was a conviction that would be sorely tested in the coming months, and it would greatly complicate the process of Carol's treatment and recovery in many ways. You could also argue it was not the most well-informed decision or the most well-thought-out either. And perhaps it wasn't. But at the same time, this decision would completely transform the next year of our lives, giving Carol's treatment and recovery all the more meaning and purpose, because we knew that at the end of it all, not only would she be cancer-free, but we would be welcoming a new life and a new member of our family into the world. It was a decision I would never, ever regret, and I believe it was the turning point of our entire story. And it all began with that not so innocent question that Dr. Griffin posed to us: "You are going to have this baby, *right*?"

Right—we will. It's funny how little it takes sometimes to get someone to do the right thing.

But before we could get too comfortable with this rather momentous decision, Dr. Griffin had another difficult question lined up for us. Without skipping a beat, she cheerily continued: "Okay! Now, if that's the case, we need to decide about surgery today. We typically don't perform surgeries like this on pregnant women because the anesthetic might harm the baby. So, we could delay the surgery until a later time to give you guys some time to figure out exactly how you want to proceed. But at the same time, you don't want to delay this surgery very long at all because Carol's tumor is aggressive. What would you like to do?"

We paused to digest what she was trying to tell us. "So . . . ," I cautiously ventured, "if we go ahead with the surgery now, there are risks to the child. But if we wait until later, there's a greater risk for Carol. Is that what you're saying?"

She nodded her head in the affirmative but continued: "Now, that being said, our anesthesiologist here is the best. I'll talk with him, but I think we can go ahead with the surgery today without harming the baby. Or at least we can minimize that risk. But you should know that there is still some risk involved. It's your decision."

Oh, how I longed for the good old days, when the most momentous decision we had to make was whether we stayed in for dinner or went out.

We didn't have much to go on to make our choice, besides the quiet confidence with which Dr. Griffin spoke, how she seemed to be somehow convinced that they could do this just right, that a balance between caring for both Carol and the baby could be reached. And so I placed two precious lives in her hands and replied, "Let's do it—let's go ahead with the surgery today. We trust you, Doctor."

She seemed touched by my response. She nodded and placed her hands on both our shoulders. And then she said something that would stick with us, even to this day: "I don't know what God is up to, but he's up to something. That's for sure!"

I could hardly argue with that.

●　●　●

Before this, I was certain I knew all the answers.

I grew up in a Catholic school, where I was one of only a handful of Asians and everyone else was Irish, with good Irish names like Colleen, Maureen, Connor, and Gavin. While I don't remember being especially spiritual or religious at the time, I do remember winning a Bible trivia contest in third grade. And that is quite strange, as I don't really recall ever reading the Bible back then. The only religious material I remember from my childhood was the book of Catholic saints, which I was morbidly drawn to because of the graphic scenes of martyrdom portrayed within.

But even from a young age, when it came to the Bible, I always knew the answers, at least the ones you were supposed to give. It was the same through high school, college, and even seminary. I had an easy facility with Scripture, could explain passages and theology in compelling ways, and people would often turn to me in that capacity, to help explain to them what God meant when he said this or that in the Bible. I was the one who knew it all, and it was this sense of comprehension that had led me to become a pastor.

I thought I knew it all. But the fact was, I knew nothing at all.

When Carol was diagnosed with triple negative, my juvenile and simplistic conception of God folded in upon itself, unable to support itself in light of the harsh reality of what life was truly like. In just one month, my view of life and of God had been quickly and totally destroyed by a quick succession of trials. And I made the rather painful realization that I didn't understand God and his ways in the least. For once in my life, I had no pat answers to explain my family's situation. It was as if an earthquake had ruined my understanding of God, and of life.

But in truth, it was not an earthquake, which is a random kind of destruction that serves no purpose. Instead, it was more like an implosion, a purposeful kind of destruction that makes room for something better to be erected in its place. My flimsy conception of God had been methodically demolished so that he could build a new one in me instead. The process of reconstruction began the moment I heard about Carol's pregnancy and that we were going to have a child. It was as if I caught a wild and brief glimpse into the sublime manner in which God really works, a new conception of his ways, one that was far beyond my ability to comprehend. Like God shouting to Job from the fury of the whirlwind, or the angel Gabriel appearing before the Virgin Mary, it was as if God was saying to me, "*Peter, look! You wanted to know what I was doing, how I work. Look, and see. I am not bound or confined by the rise and fall of circumstance. My works are far beyond your ability to understand, woven with wisdom that you do not even know of, with foresight you cannot imagine, with love so deep you cannot comprehend. My ways are higher than your ways."*

The news of this child was a revelation that God does not do things in the simplistic and fundamentally mathematical manner I had always pigeonholed him into, where good circumstances equal God, and bad circumstances do not equal God. His plans cannot be fathomed in 140 characters, and his purposes cannot be known in a single month or year or even lifetime. In other words, God does not work according to my ways or my wisdom or in my time frame—only according to his own. That day in January, a new life had been announced, but also a new understanding of God had been conceived.

But this should have been no surprise to me, because you find this same dynamic embedded in the story of salvation, the story of Jesus Christ. For example, you can almost imagine a (slightly heretical) conversation going on between angels regarding the incarnation of Christ:

Angel A: "So God wants to send a Savior, does he? Someone to bring heaven to earth and lead humanity in repentance back to God? Hallelujah!"

Angel B: "Yup."

Angel A: "It's safe, then, to assume that he will send a king or a conqueror, because that makes the most sense for that mission. Perhaps Gabriel will be sent . . . or Michael! That would be cool. I've always thought Michael the impressive sort."

Angel B: "Well, actually, I heard that God is going himself."

Angel A: "Himself, you say? Well, I suppose that could work. Job certainly got the point."

Angel B: "No, not as the whirlwind this time. Um, as a child. A baby, in fact. Born of a . . . virgin."

Angel A: *Angelic silence.* "You're kidding. And how exactly does he plan to redeem creation?"

Angel B: "Well . . . it has something to do with a crucifixion."

Angel A: *Faints in shock.*

You see, God does things his own way, not necessarily the way we think is best or can understand most clearly, and his purposes cannot be captured with crude principles and observations. But just because we fail to comprehend what he is doing does not mean he is not doing anything at all. And the sooner we accept this and put aside our simplistic and mechanistic understanding of God, the more clearly we can see God for who he truly is, and the better prepared we are for the reality of life in the world and life in Christ.

But it also wouldn't be fair to say there is no earthly rhyme or reason to God and his ways. Why would he have given us such magnificent and rational minds, unless they could be used to understand him? Every so often, in God's mercy, our minds can discern why he is doing what he is doing, and those are moments of awe-inspiring wonder. For instance, you'll recall how Carol's tumor was triple negative, meaning it would not respond to any modern hormone treatments. This was initially a huge blow to us, as it severely limited Carol's treatment options.

But it ended up being a blessing, in some strange way. Had Carol's tumor been treatable with hormone therapy, those same hormones also would have ended her pregnancy. We would have had an incredibly difficult decision: Do we give Carol those new hormone treatments and in so doing terminate the baby, or do we use some weaker treatment that would spare the child's life but endanger Carol's? There would have been no other options. But since her cancer was triple negative, it could not be treated with hormones anyway, and we were not forced to make this incredibly stark decision. Now, this did not change the fact that Carol still had a very dangerous form of breast cancer, but it was encouraging in some small way because it helped us to discern some faint outline of a plan in all of this—that perhaps God had planned all along for us to have this child. Maybe, just maybe, amidst the smoking crater of my previous life, God was at work, resetting the foundations.

With that, I watched as they wheeled Carol into surgery, and I returned to the waiting room, my thoughts and heart filled to the brim, like Mary pondering the words of Gabriel. Hours later Dr. Griffin returned to tell me that Carol's surgery had gone well and that she felt confident she had removed as much of the tumor that she could, including some lymph nodes to which the cancer had spread. I thanked her for taking such good care of my wife. But I also thank her to this very day for giving us the courage to do the right thing.

Carol was transferred to a hospital room to recover, and as she rested, I reflected on everything we had discovered that day. I realized I was as clueless as I had ever been, perhaps even more so. God's ways were no clearer to me than they had been twenty-four hours ago, and I could not comprehend what he was doing, not in the least. But at the same time, I was not anywhere near as hopeless as I had been the day before. Because even though I did not understand what God was up to, he was indeed up to something.

8

"I Don't"

Washington, D.C., is a very interesting city in many regards, not least of which is its climate. Summers are nothing short of brutal, with temperatures regularly in the nineties and humidity levels to match. What's worse, the city recently has been beset by Asian tiger mosquitoes (not to be mistaken for Asian tiger mothers), which are extremely aggressive and annoying (again, not to be mistaken for Asian tiger mothers). Unlike ordinary mosquitoes, which are active at dawn and dusk, Asian tiger mosquitoes are active at all hours, making them the world's hardest-working bloodsucking parasite. My hatred for these mosquitoes is rivaled only by my distrust of health insurance companies.

Fortunately, winters in D.C. are relatively mild, at least in comparison to the ones I experienced in Chicago as a child—that is, unless you are talking the winter of 2009–2010, otherwise known as "Snowmageddon." The D.C. area is not prone to heavy snowfall in the winter, and its residents haven't a clue how to

Sophia (on the left) and Katie enjoying Washington, D.C.,'s Snowmageddon (2010).

conduct themselves when a couple of inches of snow land on the street. At the mere threat of snow on the news, people here start driving five miles an hour with their hazard lights on, straddling two different lanes of the highway at once. But frankly, you can drive only ten miles an hour on the Beltway at the best of times. So you can imagine the city's response when forty inches of snow were dumped on the region in only a few days.

Schools shut down for weeks. Cars were trapped by the initial snowfall and then by the six-foot walls of ice created by snow plows that had driven by, ostensibly, to liberate those same cars. People cross-country skied down the middle of major streets. Snowball fights spontaneously erupted, involving hundreds of people at a time. Local police detectives took umbrage at being barraged by snowballs and drew their firearms in extreme annoyance (true story).

And our church decided to go skating at the Sculpture Garden on the National Mall.

●   ●   ●

That day in February 2010 stands out in my memory for a few reasons. First, it was one of the first days Carol was able to do physical activity of any kind since the mastectomy. Carol's mastectomy was extensive and involved removing her entire right breast as well as all the lymph nodes in her right armpit. This made her recovery process arduous. She needed to periodically drain the lymph fluid that continued to build up where her nodes used to be, a strange and alien process involving various tubes, valves, and a drainage bag. But she also had to attend physical therapy to help her deal with the damage to the muscle tissue in her chest. In this way, Snowmageddon was a blessing because Carol was forced to stay at home and rest, something she was normally loathe to do.

But by February, she finally felt well enough to venture out and come skating with us. Bundled up in a big winter coat, Carol looked just like any other person there, happy and healthy, without a care in the world and ready to have a good time. You couldn't tell that her torso was covered in bandages and a drainage tube was still connected to her body. Chemotherapy would not start for a couple of months, so her hair was still long and lustrous. I watched her skating with a mixture of thanksgiving and wistfulness, thankful she was doing well, yet yearning for the days before the diagnosis, when our lives seemed so free from such worries. But I had to admit to myself that back then, I never would have taken a moment to just watch Carol or marvel at how healthy she looked. Such blessings would have been lost on the past me. It was suffering that had taught me to pay attention and treasure the moments I normally would have let pass by without a thought.

That day I also remember giving a random toddler a bloody lip. While waiting to skate, my family made friends with the family who was standing next to us in line, a mom and her two young kids. I felt sorry for her, because taking two young children skating all by yourself is not easy, what with the tying of many laces and the losing of many gloves. My wife and I had it relatively easy, as we had friends from our church who would take turns skating with our daughters. So after a couple of guilty laps around the ice, I offered to skate with her younger child, a cute-as-a-button two-year-old boy. She seemed relieved to have the help, partially because I look relatively harmless, and partially because I am an experienced ice-skater, having played hockey as a child.

And so I took the little guy in my arms and skated with him, my hands under his armpits to help him balance, determined to make him scream with delight. He would soon scream for a different reason altogether. We were having a blast until the moment my dull rental skates got caught in an enormous gouge in the ice and I fell forward with my full weight . . . right on the boy's face. He immediately started wailing, the little pansy, his face covered in half-melted ice and blood dripping from a gash on his lip.

With a look of pure embarrassment and mortification, I handed him back to his mother, profusely apologizing for my clumsiness. All things considered, his mother took it very well, repeatedly telling me not to worry, that he fell down all the time and it didn't look too bad. I appreciated the grace with which she handled the situation but felt absolutely terrible nonetheless. Now she didn't just have to take two children skating at

Amy Walter Beisel

A day of memories—Carol finally feeling well enough after her mastectomy to go skating, and later, me bloodying the lip of a toddler when I fell trying to help him around the rink (2010).

once—she had to comfort one with a busted lip while the other incessantly asked to go back out again. In mere seconds, I had successfully made her day twice as difficult.

It was hard to bear the stares of the other skaters who had witnessed me crushing that child, and with my cheeks flushed with cold and embarrassment, I hastily exited the ice to take a walk around the Sculpture Garden. That would also make it easier to evade the police, in case the mother decided that she did want to press charges after all. I had just managed to get my mind off the little boy's bloodied visage when my phone vibrated in my pocket. I answered it, and a doctor from California greeted me. She was a preeminent oncologist who specialized in breast cancer and told me that my brother, a doctor who worked in Boston, had referred my wife's case to her. As a favor to my brother, she was calling to see if there was anything we wanted to know about this type of cancer and how it could be treated.

Recognizing what a generous gesture this was, I thanked her profusely for the call. As I paced around the Sculpture Garden, I relayed the specifics of my wife's case to her, starting with when Carol was diagnosed, the size of the tumor, and the date of surgery. Our conversation was routine until I told her that Carol was nine weeks' pregnant. At that, the doctor quickly interjected, "Wait . . . did you say 'pregnant'?"

I guess my brother had not given her *all* the details of my wife's situation. I said yes, that while getting blood tests done for her surgery, we had discovered she was six weeks' pregnant. I told her we were keeping the baby and were talking to doctors about postponing chemotherapy until Carol's second trimester in order to give the baby a better chance at survival.

She paused for a heartbeat and then, in a much more serious tone of voice, said to me, "Peter, this is not easy for me to say. But this is my advice, and just to be clear, it's the advice I would give my own sister if she were in the same situation. You should terminate this pregnancy and get started with treatment right away."

I immediately stopped walking and asked her why this was the case. She replied, "Triple negative cancer is very dangerous and kills young women at a much higher rate than other cancers. Because of this, it needs to be taken care of as quickly as possible, with absolutely no delays. If you guys wait for the baby to pass through the first trimester, that is a delay your wife may not be able to afford. If there are cancer cells in her body, it will just give them time to spread and maybe even take root somewhere else." My head started to spin. But the doctor wasn't done yet.

"Moreover, I don't know if anyone has told you this, but the recommended chemotherapy drugs that triple negative patients should receive have not been proven safe for a developing fetus." This was a surprise to me. None of the other doctors we had spoken to had brought this up. "Now, you could pick other drugs that have proven safe for a fetus, but they are not nearly as effective against triple negative. So taking this route will only hurt your wife, because chemotherapy is really your only means of treating triple negative. Again, I really want you to know that this is what I would tell my own family, my own sister: You should abort this pregnancy."

I tried my best to keep up with the technical details that she shared with me—about the different types of chemicals used in chemotherapy and the survival rates based on the speed of treatment, ideas difficult enough to digest under calmer circumstances. Still, I understood the gist of what she said. If we made any efforts to keep this baby, my wife's health would be compromised. But if we went ahead with immediate and aggressive treatment, my child's health would be compromised as well—more than that, it likely would be ended altogether.

The question before us was a bleak one: Should we prioritize the survival of my wife or the life of our unborn child? Dare I take a risk with the health of my wife, the mother of our two daughters? Was it fair to allow our unborn child to develop amidst caustic chemicals that might cause him or her great harm? How does one even begin to make such choices?

Even though it had been only a few weeks since Carol's surgery and the powerful revelation that God was up to something,

I had a sudden relapse. A sensation of cold fear gripped me, and terribly familiar questions flooded my mind: *Why, God? Why are you doing this to us? What have we done to deserve this? Why did you give my wife cancer just after we planted a church that we believed you wanted us to start? Why did you give her a form of cancer as aggressive as this? And why did you give us this baby, only for us to have to terminate it immediately afterward? It just doesn't make any sense!*

Why do you do things for no reason?!

I stood still in the garden, overwhelmed, my fear and sadness juxtaposed with the sound of children laughing and playing in the distance. My brother's friend, knowing what must be going through my mind, remained respectfully quiet on the other end of the line. Standing there, my phone pressed tightly against the sweaty side of my head, I felt completely and utterly alone. And I know this sounds strange, but I swear that in that bleak moment, as I stood in the Sculpture Garden of the National Mall, I heard God answer:

"I don't, Peter. I always have a reason."

I froze as this thought worked its way through my mind. Perhaps he hadn't given us this child for no reason. Maybe, even though this excellent doctor and I could not begin to understand it, God had a plan for everything we had endured so far. Maybe this baby was no accident and nothing I should abandon, even with great reason. I suddenly felt much better, even calm, peaceful. I thought to myself, *God does all things with purpose—it's just that I can't see that purpose yet.*

After a long silence, the doctor patiently asked if I had any questions for her. I reflected for a moment and told her that Carol had only a little over one month left until her first trimester was done and asked if a delay of four or five weeks would have that much impact on Carol's recovery. She acquiesced that it might not, but it would be best not to take chances, not with triple negative cancer. But she reminded me that was not the only issue to consider; even if we did wait to start chemotherapy, the chemotherapy recommended for Carol's cancer was not proven safe on pregnant women and might harm the child. Therefore, it would be better to terminate the pregnancy immediately.

This second argument struck me as strange, so I doubled back and posed some more questions. I asked what it meant, exactly, that the drug had "not been proven safe," and she said that it did not mean it was necessarily harmful, only that clinical studies had not yet proven it was safe. So I asked, "So, let's say there is some chance the baby could have some problems when he or she is born because of the chemotherapy. That's not any worse than terminating the baby, right?"

There was a pause, and the doctor said she didn't understand what I was getting at. And so I tried to explain my reasoning in another way.

"You said that because the drug has not been proven safe for a fetus, it is better to terminate the pregnancy. But surely termination would be worse for the fetus than taking our chances with a drug that has not been proven safe clinically. Nothing could be more unsafe for the child than to abort it. Couldn't we just wait for four weeks and start Carol on the chemotherapy regimen that is recommended for her? That way Carol would be getting the best chemo for her, and the baby would also get a chance as well."

She paused again to process my convoluted logic and went on to say that although she understood what I was getting at, as a doctor, she could not recommend that course of action. There were just too many risks and unknowns involved. She reiterated again that her professional advice was for immediate abortion, followed by chemotherapy. I understood her point and told her so, and that I would share all of this information with Carol, and I thanked her wholeheartedly for her time and consideration.

As Carol and I drove home from skating that afternoon, I talked to her about my conversation and the advice the doctor had given us. Because this affected Carol and her health most significantly, I didn't want to affect her decision in any way, so I tried to present the choices in as neutral of a way as I could.

After I finished, she didn't say anything for a long time, which I totally understood, given the magnitude of the decision before us. But after a few minutes of silence, I asked her what she thought.

"What do you mean?" she replied.

"What do you think about what the doctor said? What do you think we should do about the baby?"

"Oh. I think we should keep the baby, of course. Isn't that what we decided when Dr. Griffin told us?"

"Yes . . . ," I cautiously ventured, realizing where this was going and not liking it.

"That's what I thought too. So I think I should go ahead with the standard treatment, but just wait until the second trimester. That way the baby gets a better chance and I'll get the standard care." She looked at me curiously, as if trying to understand what my problem was.

My problem was that I saw faith and conviction in a starkly different light from my wife. For Carol, faith is believing wholeheartedly in a conviction and sticking with it no matter what. She felt convicted that God had given us this child, so she was going to keep the child, simple as that. Any possible future debate would be addressed by that prior conviction. She has, you know, *real faith.*

For me, faith is all too often believing in something 50 percent and then constantly questioning and revisiting that decision time and time again, doubting whether I made the right choice or heard God correctly. This is due to the fact that my faith is more often than not tied to my comprehension, which is a pretty flimsy and capricious foundation, when you think about it. What's so ironic is that I do all of this hand-wringing to avoid suffering, when this tendency almost always makes my life far worse. I destroy myself with constant indecision and end up making terrible snap judgments based on the tiniest and feeblest impressions. We are very different, my wife and I, but perhaps in no way more clearly than this: She is a woman of great faith, and I am a man of . . . other gifts. But when you think about it, perhaps my faith is actually greater than hers, given that it comes so unnaturally to me. That's what I like to tell myself at least.

A few days later, we talked the situation over with Carol's oncologist at Georgetown and agreed to pursue a unique course of treatment. We would wait until Carol's first trimester was completed to begin chemotherapy so that the baby had a better chance at survival. And then we would begin chemotherapy using the same drugs she would have received even if she were not pregnant. That way Carol would have a better chance at survival as well. Were we taking a gamble with Carol's life, as well as the baby's? Yes, I have to admit that to no small degree, we were. We did not make this decision flippantly or without fully taking into account the risks. But we did make this decision in faith, believing that if we tried our best to safeguard and preserve both Carol and the baby, God would take care of them both—believing that God had given us this child for a reason.

Later I called my brother to tell him what his friend had shared with me and what Carol and I had decided in turn.

He listened quietly and then said soberly, "Peter, as a doctor, I probably would agree with my friend. But as your brother, I want you to know that I think you're doing the right thing. I know you can't always do things by the book, and you have to take a chance sometimes. And this is a chance that you have to take." This encouraged me a great deal, that such an experienced doctor and caring brother would understand the risks we were taking, but also why we felt we had to take them. This was our plan, our conviction, and we would follow it to the end.

●　●　●

To some, this plan still may not seem very sound. We had just been told by a preeminent breast cancer specialist that Carol's chances at survival would be negatively affected if we kept this child. When viewed in this light, this child could have just as easily been seen as a curse, not a blessing. What made us so certain this pregnancy was a gift from God that we had to protect, even at great cost? That's a good question, one I wrestled with daily. And what I came up with is that sometimes you don't even have to look at a gift to know that it is good. *All you have to know is who gave it to you.*

A good example of this comes from an Advent story, Jesus' presentation at the temple from Luke 2. When Jesus is presented at the temple, a devout old man named Simeon rises to meet him. And through the insight of the Holy Spirit, Simeon immediately recognizes that Jesus is nothing less than the Christ, the Messiah sent by God. Simeon embraces the child, praising God that he was able to lay eyes on the Christ, even going so far as to say that now he can die in peace. As a result of human beings' inherent distaste for their own demise, very rarely are people truly at peace about dying. So something truly amazing must have happened in that moment for Simeon to utter such a thing.

The question is, *what exactly did Simeon see that day?* Did a divine sheen surround Jesus, or did Jesus make the sign of the cross with his chubby little fingers? From what we can see in the passage, the answer is no. Jesus performs no miracle of any kind, nor was there a Nativity-like chorus of angels that burst into song or a bright star that curiously hovered overhead, diverted from its ordinary trajectory. At this point, Jesus must have seemed like an ordinary baby and little more.

But if Jesus didn't do anything special, or didn't appear outwardly special in any way, why does Simeon react as if he does, as if he had just witnessed a profound miracle of the highest degree? I think this can be partly explained by the ministry of the Holy Spirit, that it was the Holy Spirit who brought Simeon to Jesus and revealed Jesus' true identity to him. What a reminder that we need the Spirit to see Jesus clearly!

The passage also explains that Simeon had been a devout and righteous man his entire life. And being a man who knows God well, who knows that God is both good and loving, Simeon knew that whomever God sent to Israel would be good and loving as well. So in this sense, he didn't need to see Jesus do anything amazing to know that he was amazing. Because Simeon trusted the Giver, he was able to see the Gift, Jesus, for what he truly was.

If this story feels too distant, consider a more modern Christmastime analogy: white elephant gift exchanges. In this more contemporary Christmas tradition, everyone brings a present, the contents of which are a secret. Without knowing what is inside, each person picks a present and opens it and then, if they like it, scheme of ways to hold on to it. If they don't like it, they scheme of ways to get rid of it in exchange for something better.

I have played this game many times in my life and invariably leave the party with something purchased at Starbucks—it never fails.

The trick of the game is to initially use any means necessary to discern what might be inside. You can look at the quality of the wrapping, or the size of the present, but neither of these necessarily indicates that what is inside is a quality gift. Sometimes people will wrap terrible gifts in elaborate boxes in order to disguise what's within, like the time I put a bag of Oreo cookies in a box that used to contain an Xbox video game console.

No, one of the best ways to figure out if a gift is going to be good is to figure out who brought it. If one of your friends is legendary for his generosity and for wildly exceeding the dollar limit usually set for these gift exchanges, *you should pick his gift*—even if it's small or wrapped in a brown paper bag, the wrapping technique of choice for many men like me. No, you may not know what's inside. But since you know who's giving it, you can be certain it's something good.

So it is with God. Because of our incredibly limited wisdom and comprehension, very rarely will we be able to grasp the true worth of that which God gives us. More often than not, we look at those gifts with confusion, even horror, wondering why God has given us something that differs so starkly from what we asked him for. This is in many ways what Jesus was to the people of Israel. They had hoped for a political liberator who would lead them in revolt against their Roman oppressors. Instead, they were given a humble son of a carpenter, who preached nonviolence and forgiveness. The disappointment the people of Israel would experience was so acute it would eventually lead them to demand that a murderer be released to them instead of Jesus.

In times like that, when we can't comprehend what God is doing, like my afternoon in the Sculpture Garden, we have to take our eyes off the gift and focus instead on the Giver. We should remember what it says in James 1:17, that every good and perfect gift comes from our heavenly Father, and also what Jesus teaches on prayer in Luke 11, that even our earthly fathers know better than to give us a snake or scorpion if we ask for bread. How much more, then, our Father in heaven? If we can remember such truths in those moments, it is far easier to look at the gift on our lap and recognize it for its true and priceless worth, even though it may be wrapped in dirty rags or born in a manger.

Or if you find out about it right before going in for major surgery.

The Seminary of Suffering

During this difficult season, our friends were nothing short of amazing. They cooked our meals, babysat our children, and prayed for us unceasingly. A number of them even pitched in to buy Carol an exercise machine so she could keep active throughout treatment. They were beyond generous and willing to support us in any way possible. They would do anything for us.

They just didn't know what to *say* to us.

Many friends e-mailed us their condolences, and it was clear that most of them did not know where to start, or what was appropriate. One good friend of ours, God bless her, sent us a confident and aggravatingly cheery e-mail that proclaimed, "You're going to get through this, no problem!!! I just know that Carol is going to be healed, and God is going to do something awesome out of this!!!" Here's a word of advice to everyone: Don't say this to someone who just found out they have cancer. Even if true in some deeper theological sense, it's really not all that helpful. In fact, when e-mailing them, it's better to just avoid the use of exclamation points altogether.

Another good friend came over to our house to drop off dinner for our family, a delicious roasted chicken garnished with onions, potatoes, and carrots. We thanked her for her generosity and fell into conversation for a few minutes. Our time started off well enough, but the more we talked, the clearer it became that she was not holding up well. Her voice shook, and she had difficulty looking either of us squarely in the eye. Eventually she dissolved into tears before us, while Carol and I looked at each other in amazement.

Carol gave me a questioning look, as if to ask what we should do. I simply shrugged my shoulders. I didn't really know how to comfort someone because they had failed to comfort someone else. So Carol tentatively inched closer to our friend and, laying her hand gently upon her shoulder, soothed, "There, there, it will all be okay, really! You'll see—I'll be fine." Sniffling, our friend gratefully placed her hand on Carol's and nodded in agreement, while I tried vainly to suppress the sardonic smile that crept onto my face. Evidently, it was grueling work to comfort a person who had cancer.

I don't say this to fault any of our friends, not in the least. We love them deeply and could easily recognize that although their attempts to comfort us were at times clumsy, they were incredibly sincere. Their responses were not caused by a lack of care, but a lack of experience. They simply had never known anyone who had breast cancer so they did not know what to say in that situation. And it was no different for Carol and me, as we ourselves did not know a single other person in our age group who had breast cancer. It was not a common experience for thirty-somethings, and that lack of experience translated into an inability to comprehend and to comfort.

As a result, we began to feel increasingly frightened and isolated by our situation. It was hard not to feel that way, when close friends spontaneously burst into tears at the sight of us or stuttered in their attempts to find the right words to comfort us. The people who were closest to us understood us the least. But whatever they said, it was clear they pitied us and our sorry situation, and so inevitably, we began to pity ourselves as well.

But not everyone treated us this way. My neighbor across the street, Joe, had a very different response from my friends. Joe is an old codger in the best possible sense. Early every morning, I would watch as he strapped on his fanny pack and headed out to the local thrift shops and swap meets to buy used lawn mowers to add to his collection of a half dozen or more that he stored in caches throughout his basement and backyard. Once he saw me futilely trying to cut the grass with a manual push mower and gave me one of his electric mowers instead. I was deeply thankful for his generosity, even though the mower left behind a trail of rust every time I tried to use it, before eventually collapsing on itself in a mushroom cloud of brownish-red dust.

Joe loved to tell me stories of the bad old days in the city, when drug crews were armed with assault rifles and dead bodies would turn up in the park across the street. With a bewildering sense of wistfulness, he would regale me with stories of how his wife had stumbled upon a corpse while walking the dog a few years ago, or how they had arranged their house so that their bedroom faced away from the street in order to protect themselves against common and random gunfire. I got the strangest sense that although he would never want to go back to that state of life, he recalled it with some fondness. It's funny how the human mind works, that we sometimes can look back warmly on parts of our lives that can only be described as hellishly difficult.

Actually, I can relate.

In one passing conversation with Joe, I broke the news that Carol had cancer and half expected him to heap pity on us, or make some excuse to walk away, like many people we had told so far. But he didn't. Instead, with compassion, and yet without batting an eye, he replied, "Oh, that's too bad. Is she doing well and feeling strong?" That might not seem like that helpful of a response, but it was not what he said, but how he said it—with definite concern, but not shock or horror. I had never heard anyone respond to our news this way and was taken aback by his levelness.

When I responded that she was doing pretty well, he enthused, "That's good! Make sure she exercises and gets lots of rest." He straightened up and put his hands on his hips, proudly declaring, "My prostate cancer is in remission right now, and I feel great! I'm walking and working. I'm sure she'll be up and around in no time." A thought apparently came to him suddenly, and he told me to wait right there in his driveway. I watched as he puttered back to his house and returned with a copy of Elizabeth Edwards's autobiography, which describes her own fight with breast cancer. He pressed the book into my hands and urged me to take it to my wife. I thanked him and walked away, feeling a strange sense of equanimity. Joe made me feel like our situation, although bad, was not a disaster.

My other neighbor, Sheila, responded in a similar fashion. Sheila was as equally cool as Joe—a bubbling woman of infinite joy and hope with a laugh so explosive it would often startle our children and me as well. When I told her about Carol's cancer, her normally ebullient face immediately fell. But her melancholy was short-lived and quickly transitioned to a kind of eager helpfulness. With animated resolve, she said, "Okay. So what do y'all need? You need me to look after the girls or the house? I can get my son to mow your lawn. You need anything, just let me know!"

My eyes widened, not just because she was speaking so loudly, but because of her positivity and eagerness. Laughing, I told her we would let her know. But to be honest, I knew that I could never bring myself to ask for her help. I was well aware of what she was going through in her own life and that she was scarcely in any position to sacrifice for my family. She had been unemployed for six months and was finding it difficult to provide for her two sons and her ailing mother, who was suffering from the late stages of dementia.

Sheila's story was pretty typical of most people who lived around us. This person's mother and sister had both died of breast cancer. An uncle had lost a foot and then both legs to diabetes. This son had been lost to drugs and gangs, another to alcohol. And everywhere, unemployment. But because of these relationships and experiences, our neighbors instinctively knew how to respond to the news of Carol's cancer—with sincerity, evenness, and a commitment to helping in any simple way they could. It was their deep familiarity with suffering in all its forms that made them such effective comforters. They had mourned, and they knew how to comfort the mourning in turn. Their expertise in counseling came not through formal schooling in the subject, but through the school of hard knocks, or what I call the seminary of suffering, where you earn your MIS, or master's in suffering.

It is not a degree I ever wanted, but it is the one I now use the most as a pastor.

● ● ●

To add to everything else that was transpiring in our lives, I was also supposed to be planting a church. As you can imagine, it wasn't exactly my first priority, given everything else that was going on. But neither was it far from the front of my mind. I had been thinking and dreaming about this church for years, and some portion of my identity as a pastor had become tangled up with this endeavor. Any time and energy that wasn't being invested into Carol and the girls went to the church, meeting with members, putting together sermons and events, and planning our calendar.

This last part was of vital importance. Carol's treatments were scheduled to begin in April of 2010, after which I would have precious little bandwidth to devote to the church. So I had devised a plan to get the church up and running at full steam before then. If we could get off to a strong-enough start, the church would have momentum of its own, allowing me to shift my focus to taking care of Carol and the family instead. It was an excellent plan, worked out to the very day. And when we launched the church, we did have momentum of a sort.

Negative momentum, that is.

Our first official service was on April 4, 2010—Easter Sunday, the last Sunday before Carol's treatments began. We felt like that would be the perfect day to launch a new church, as people would naturally be looking for one to attend. Moreover, there was something so fitting about opening a church on a day that celebrated the resurrection of Christ. All the details had been worked out: We would serve lamb for lunch after service—again, very appropriate, given the season. One of our members would share her powerful personal testimony of how she had lost her father to violent crime, but also how God had brought a sense of peace back into her life. And I planned on wearing my good tan suit, which I had bought specifically for that day. It was going to be awesome. I was especially excited about the suit, as all my other suits were black or dark blue. But at least they matched.

Even before we started the service, we found ourselves on shaky ground. A decent number of people had shown up, but still far fewer than I was hoping for. This was not encouraging. To make things even worse, little Katie was being an absolute terror, a role she rarely played. Her mouth firmly set into a comically deep frown, she complained incessantly and insisted on wrapping herself around my leg, which made it intensely difficult for me to focus on the service. As a result, a few butterflies fluttered around in my gut. But I swatted them away and assured myself, *It's okay! There are still new people here, and we can get started with them! And Katie's just being a brat; she'll be fine too.* I convinced myself it was still going to be awesome.

We started our service, got through our time of praise, and that was my cue. I bounded up in front of the congregation, wearing my awesome tan suit, and enthusiastically welcomed

Our first service at Riverside and my brand-new tan suit.

everyone to the official launch of Riverside Covenant Church. I shared the vision of our community, that we wanted to be a church where spirituality and mission were in healthy balance with one another. And to that end, a sister would be coming up to share her own testimony of how God had healed her and her family from a terrible personal tragedy.

I invited my friend up to the stage to share, and . . . nothing. No one came forward. I looked about the room but didn't see her face anywhere. The butterflies came back with a vengeance in that moment, filling my stomach and tickling the bottom of my throat. And only seconds before the silence that filled the room could become a crushing black hole of awkwardness, I quickly apologized that the testimony was not ready and asked instead if people would bow their heads for prayer, which would give me a quick moment to gather myself.

With my eyes closed, I stuffed down the butterflies with both hands and focused all my attention on giving the best sermon that I could. At least that would be awesome—that and, of course, the suit. And so I launched into the sermon about forgiveness that I had crafted for the day The main thrust of the message was that we are far more likely to forgive those we love, which means that God must love us quite a bit to forgive us of so much and so often.

The sermon was going quite well, and I was starting to regain some of the momentum that had been lost earlier in the service. I had just hit a crucial part of my message when I started to hear this quiet but insistent beeping in the background. *Beep—beep—beep.* The noise threw me off, and the butterflies mounted their assault. I tried my best to soldier on, but the beeping continued from somewhere inside the building. I tried to ignore it for a little while more but finally blurted out, "What is that sound?" At that precise moment, as if scripted by a team of ham-fisted Hollywood comedy writers, the fire alarm began blasting throughout the entire building, the result of the Easter lamb that was burning in the kitchen upstairs. It turns out, this is why my friend had not been there to give her testimony; she had been frantically opening windows and trying to fan the smoke detector into silence. I shouted above the din that everyone should head outside until the fire trucks arrived.

Killer butterflies fluttered victoriously over my bloated corpse.

Thankfully, shock and trauma left me with little memory of the rest of the service, only that it was the worst service I had ever been a part of and, unfortunately, the official start of our church. My only goal in life was to get this miserable day over so I could go home and totally forget the day had ever occurred. And so after the fire department came and left, I blew through the rest of the sermon, didn't eat a bite of the lamb that had so effectively sabotaged the service, and without a word drove home with my family. Katie, who had been so whiny all morning, began to look more miserable and pale with every minute, and the moment we pulled up in front of our house, the poor thing threw up all over herself and the interior of the car.

I never wore that tan suit ever again.

In retrospect, this story is funny to me, albeit in a cringe-inducing sort of way. But at that time, this debacle had a profoundly negative effect on me. In a period of no more than three hours, my elaborate plan for the launch of the church had been torched, like so much burned lamb chop. I was hoping we would have momentum and excitement going into this difficult season of life, but instead, my team and I were left with little more than the memory of a catastrophe. And worse, Carol would have to start her chemotherapy sessions, and I would be left to try to cobble something together that resembled a healthy, functioning church.

I tried to bravely soldier on from that moment, but the truth was, as a pastor, I had lost much of my enthusiasm and nearly all of my confidence. My faith in God was undergoing a huge shift, my theology completely imploding on itself. My attention was constantly split between issues of huge significance—cancer, pregnancy, family, church—issues too titanic for any one individual to address adequately. I had never planted a church before, much less attempted to plant one when my wife was seriously ill and pregnant, and neither had anyone else I knew. I felt lost and alone, walking into a difficult season of life for which I had no precedent and few friends who could truly understand or give me practical guidance.

It's a little embarrassing to admit, but because of this, I didn't put much effort into trying to get more people to attend our church. In fact, I genuinely felt bad for people who did wander through our doors, wondering if they had any idea how fragile the pastor in front was and if they might be better served elsewhere. I think I might have even told them as much.

Despite my ambivalence, I began to notice that certain kinds of people were naturally attracted to our ministry. It wasn't the typical person you see at church plants, the highly energetic and opinionated young Christian with lots of ideas and enthusiasm. No, we instead began to see the opposite—people who were doing quite badly in one way or another . . . much like myself. All were burned out, spiritually and physically. Some had wandered far from God and did not think a way back to him could be made. Some suffered physically, from cancer, from infertility. Some were mourning the loss of friends and family. Some suffered from mental illness of varying degrees—depression, postpartum issues, bipolar disorder. And that included one special young woman who came to our church in those months, a woman named Meg.

As I did with most newcomers at church, I asked Meg if she wanted to have lunch together so that I could answer any questions she might have about the church. She said yes, and we decided to meet at Union Station, in a strangely quiet corner of that behemoth structure. Over lunch, Meg told me a little about herself, that she had come to the city to do nonprofit work, a common narrative for young people in D.C. But as we talked, I couldn't help but notice that both her voice and hands trembled constantly. Then I caught a brief glimpse of her forearms, which had been hidden by the long sleeves of her shirt. Hatch marks of thin, pale scars crisscrossed her flesh, some of those lines still red and raw.

She must have seen me catch a glimpse of her scars, because as if to forestall my questions, she stopped what she was saying and suddenly interjected, "I should tell you that I am bipolar. I've been suffering from it ever since I was a teenager." She paused, and seeing that I had nothing to say in response, she explained her condition in more detail: the swings in emotion and in energy, the periods of intense creativity and enthusiasm, followed by periods of extreme depression. She told me about the myriad drugs she had been prescribed through her life, which caused side effects like shaking hands. She also told me about the cutting and how she would inflict pain on herself as a way of making herself feel something—anything at all. And she told me about the suicide attempts and how every birthday that she celebrated was something of a miracle.

I listened quietly, trying to gather the right words to say in response to this deluge of rather frightening information. But there were none. So when she was done, I asked simply and directly, "Meg, why did you pick our church of all places to come to? We're so small, and we really don't have much to offer when it comes to counseling or professional resources. Why us?"

She reflected for a moment, then replied, "Well, I guess it was *you*. I knew you would understand because of your own situation. Honestly, if you weren't going through what you were going through, I never would have come to this church." I was taken aback. It was not my degree or my sermons that had brought her to our church or qualified me as a minister in her eyes. It was the fact that I was suffering, like she was. She knew I was a fellow co-sufferer and so would understand where she was coming from. And strangely, despite my limited exposure to bipolar, I really did.

Meg and I got to know one another quite well during the summer of 2010. She was far from her family and did not like the therapist she was seeing at that time, so I became one of the main people she turned to for support during that season. She taught me about mental health and the fundamental misunderstandings people have about mental illness, and I shared my thoughts from a Christian pastoral position, something she had not heard in a while.

Through our conversations, I came to realize that those who suffer from severe mental illness are some of the strongest and bravest people walking the planet. Life can be a struggle for all of us, even in the best of situations. But those who have mental illness also shoulder the burden of persistent and unexplainable feelings of depression, suicidal thoughts, and paranoia. In some ways, it is like swimming in rough seas, only with a fifty-pound weight attached to your belt. Anyone who survives that is a hero in my book, but sadly, the mentally ill are labeled as pariahs instead.

One day Meg and I were having one of our regular conversations, and it was clear that she was not doing very well. She didn't like her new therapist, and their unproductive sessions together had made Meg particularly irritable. I tried my best to listen intently, but Sophia was home from school and, in the manner of four-year-olds everywhere, was simultaneously begging me to turn on a video, open a granola bar wrapper, and read a book to her. Using my shoulders to press my phone to my ear, fingers tugging at a greasy granola bar wrapper, I apologized to Meg. "Listen, I'm sorry about this, but I have to run. The girls are driving me up the wall—"

Meg was usually very accommodating in these situations, but this time, before I could even finish my apology, she said in a shrill voice, "If you leave this conversation right now, I don't know what will happen."

At first, I was shocked by her response, maybe even a little put off. But this was not the first time I had heard someone use this kind of voice.

I had heard this kind of voice before, from the woman on the road in Connecticut, from my wife after her diagnosis, and in the desperate prayers I poured out to God in my basement. I was familiar with that voice, the voice of real brokenness, and could hear that Meg was emotionally on the edge of a dark place.

This time I knew how to respond. I calmly replied, "Sure, Meg, no problem. Let's talk some more." And that's exactly what we did. Had I blown her off or been annoyed at her attitude and cut our conversation short, I don't know what would have happened. This might sound dramatic, but there is a chance that would have been the last time I or anyone else heard from Meg. Instead, we were able to talk through that difficult moment and end our conversation on a peaceful and stable note. And we would have many good conversations afterward, until she moved away to be closer to family.

I knew what to say in that moment and how to say it, not by virtue of any counseling courses that I had taken in seminary, or anything to that effect. Rather, it was the other and more costly degree that enabled me to empathize with Meg that day: my master's in suffering. It was the fear and brokenness and sadness that I had been wrestling with in my own life that allowed me to identify those same emotions in the voice of another. My growing familiarity with suffering and brokenness was forging me into a far better pastor.

That is not to say that I was a bad pastor before this. I suppose I was a competent one, perhaps a good one in some ways. But before this particular season of my life, my authority as a minister was primarily derived from knowledge and skills. I am a good speaker, a good musician, and a good teacher. And because of these abilities, I was a good pastor . . . or so I thought.

But there was a major problem in all of this: The gospel cannot be comprehended in its fullest form through knowledge or skill alone. You see, you cannot truly understand the gospel and the depth of God's love unless you understand suffering. Suffering lies at the root of the history of Israel. It permeates the life of Christ and the disciples and the early church. Suffering is the very reason Jesus comes to us in the first place. You cannot divorce suffering from the gospel.

But you also can't really *teach* someone to understand suffering. There is nothing you can read or study or hear that can ever fully communicate the depth and breadth of what it feels like to suffer. You can watch a great movie about someone losing someone close to them, or someone suffering from depression, but that movie will pale in comparison to the feeling of actual loss, to the personal helplessness of depression. You can study economics and the markets and all that, but that doesn't mean you know what it feels like to be unemployed or foreclosed on or homeless, not in the least. There are no academic degrees in suffering, only battle scars. Pain can be truly understood only by those who have endured it themselves. Neither can you be truly compassionate unless you have suffered. Compassion is not simply feeling bad for another human being—that is the definition of *sympathy*. No, the literal definition of compassion is to actually suffer with someone, alongside of them. And so how can someone who has not truly suffered ever display true compassion?

That was my greatest failing as a pastor—that I had never truly suffered. And because I was unfamiliar with true suffering, mourning, loss, and failure, I could not understand the heart of the gospel, which deals with suffering, mourning, loss, and failure. I could not be truly compassionate and utter those priceless and painful words: "I know exactly what you are going through." It was not from lack of trying or desire or education, but from lack of experience. I simply could not understand a gospel of suffering because I did not know suffering myself.

But as I became more and more personally acquainted with disappointment and pain, my knowledge and appreciation of the life of Jesus began to grow deeper as well. I found that I could truly relate to the story of the Annunciation, when the angel Gabriel suddenly announces that Mary is pregnant with the Son of God. We had a similar moment of mind-exploding shock before Carol's mastectomy, and we marveled at the calmness and submission in Mary's response: "Let it be to me as you have said."

Likewise, the Nativity had a newfound personal connection to me, because I know what it is like for a child to bring great hope into great darkness. I could relate to Jesus and the adulation that followed him in his first years of ministry because I had experienced the same with my church plant and the stark juxtaposition with what would follow that season.

And I finally understood the cross.

I remember officiating the Lord's Supper right after Carol's surgery. My wife had baked a challah for the occasion, a beautiful bread that is knotted and tied almost like muscles and ligaments of the human body. And during Communion, as my hands split the bread, I said, "This is my body, which is broken for you." And right there, the words had weight and meaning that they never had had before. A few weeks ago in surgery, my wife's body had been cut open, her cancer cut out and dealt with, giving her a new lease on life. Carol forever carries the scars of that moment on her body. In the same way, on the cross, Jesus' body was broken, and sin was dealt with, by his sacrifice, by his blood. He bears the scars of that moment as well. As my hands tore the knotted bread in two, I thought of my wife and thought of my Savior. I simultaneously mourned and celebrated the brokenness that results in new life, the gospel of Christ in its purest form.

Today I am not the same pastor I was before all of this took place. Suffering has, in many ways, crushed into dust all the things I previously found confidence in as a pastor. I am less certain of myself and more aware of how fragile my own strengths and skills are, as well as those of others. I don't really have "dreams" any longer, at least not related to ministry. I have seen firsthand how dangerous it is to place your hopes in a dream, because dreams can quickly turn into debacles. And what was the point of having ambition for the future, as if we could somehow guarantee our futures even beyond a single day? That's like building a towering sand castle close to the water's edge, with the tide rushing in.

Suffering has taken many things from me but given many back in return. It has given me unparalleled insight into the heart of the gospel—why Jesus came and what he went through to make all things new. The sacrifice of Christ and his victory became so real, so powerful, and so very necessary. It has forged me into a more compassionate human being and a better listener. My preaching is not as impressive as it may have been, erudite and filled with trenchant insight. Now it is personal and simple, birthed primarily out of my family's personal experiences in the valley of the shadow of death. And because of this, after everything that we have gone through, I don't think I'm done doing ministry.

In fact, I feel like I am just getting started.

The Mulberry and the Wisteria

Before Carol's chemotherapy treatment could begin, she would have to have a port installed. A "port" sounds benign enough and brings to my mind the charming little day trips you can purchase while on a cruise ship. Or else those charming little windows that you use to look out of a cruise ship. That's not what Carol's port was.

Hers was a piece of medical hardware that would be surgically implanted into her upper chest, jutting out of her skin like something out of the movie *The Matrix*. It allowed chemotherapy drugs to be more easily injected into her jugular for quick dispersal throughout her body. So, yeah, nothing to do with cruise ships. But as horrific as all that sounds, the installation of her port was supposed to be a relatively easy process, which is why I had brought our daughters with me to pick up their mother from Georgetown Hospital.

But from the moment I saw Carol that afternoon, I could tell she was not feeling well. The anesthetic that had been used for the procedure had made Carol feel terribly nauseous, which was compounded by the queasiness that she already was experiencing from being three months' pregnant.

We left the doctor's office and headed for the parking lot, walking at a snail's pace, as anything faster would run the risk of making her throw up. Our walk took us down one of the main corridors of the university's student center, the Leavey Center. It was lunchtime, and young undergraduates milled around us. They regarded our slow-moving caravan with curiosity, a nauseous-looking woman staggering down the hall, flanked by her two little girls and concerned husband. Carol's eyes were fixed firmly on the floor, where flip-flops and boat shoes abounded. Although in the same hallway, my family and those undergraduates lived in two completely separate worlds: theirs, fast-paced and unburdened, and ours, one in which time and people moved more slowly, hampered by sober realities they had not yet experienced and so could not understand.

We had not gone more than a few dozen feet before Carol, overwhelmed by an especially intense wave of nausea, stopped to lean against the wall. Carol stood silent and motionless for more than a minute as Sophia and Katie watched her with wide eyes. Finally, no longer able to take it, Carol plunged her hand into her bag and whipped out the large travel mug she was carrying and vomited inside.

When she was done, I guided her into a nearby stairwell so she could sit down and rest without having to endure the stares of every bewildered undergrad who passed us by. Knowing there was little I could do to make her feel better physically, I put my hand on Carol's shoulder and gave it a squeeze and told her that I would try to get us home as quickly as possible. Carol nodded weakly and even ventured a smile. My words clearly made her feel better . . . or else it was the fact that she had just thrown up. Probably the latter.

But sensing little eyes on us, I turned to our daughters and explained to them that even though Mommy was feeling very sick, she was really okay. We just had to get her home so that she could rest. "And then everything will be fine—I promise," I assured them. They nodded, visibly comforted by their confidence that whatever their father said would certainly come to pass, a confidence I hardly shared.

Even though I was surrounded by my family, I suddenly felt very alone while standing in that stairwell. I desperately wished that someone bigger and stronger could do the same for me: put a hand on my shoulder and tell me everything would be okay. God knows I could have used the kind word at that moment. But I would hear no such thing, not that day. Instead, a question came to mind that filled me with dread: If this was only the procedure to get her ready for chemotherapy, *what would chemotherapy itself be like?*

●　　●　　●

Carol's first day of her chemotherapy was only a week later. I wanted to be by her side during the treatments, especially for the first one. But because they took place in the afternoon, and I had to be at home to take care of Katie and pick up Sophia from school, that wasn't possible. And so I was forced to drop Carol off at the hospital to endure her first day of chemo by herself, a fact that pained me deeply. Afterward, I tried to go about my business, taking care of church matters and the like, but I was constantly plagued by the thought of Carol at the hospital without anyone at her side. I told myself I had no choice, that someone had to stay home to take care of the kids, but this had no effect. We like to think ourselves as logical creatures, and that necessity is all we require to have a sense of perspective on a difficult situation. Necessity may be nice, but it is still not enough to stave off feelings of guilt and self-reproach. Just ask any parent who is forced to work when they would prefer to be at home with their kids.

I felt so miserable about this that I decided we should celebrate Carol's first day of treatment by all going out to dinner. So I packed my daughters into the minivan and headed to Georgetown to pick Carol up from the hospital. When she walked out of the Lombardi Center, the cancer wing of the hospital, I was surprised that she seemed okay, the same as when I had first dropped her off. Strangely, I had assumed the side effects of the chemo would be evident from the outset, as if her hair would fall out all at once. Little did I know that the effects are cumulative, stacking on top of one another, meaning every subsequent treatment would be more difficult than the last, which is in some way a fitting metaphor for life itself.

After she sat down in the passenger side seat, I leaned over to give her a big hug, but then hesitated. I was afraid she might be sore from the injections or nauseous from the medications, so I settled on giving her an awkward but extremely heartfelt pat on the shoulder. I told her I had arranged for all of us to have dinner at a nice restaurant not too far away from Georgetown, which seemed to cheer her immensely. The thought of good food has always had that effect on my wife.

But the truth was, I was in no mood to celebrate. While driving to the restaurant, I was stressed and distracted, my mind still crammed with thoughts about Carol, my daughters, the baby, chemotherapy, the church—and *WHAM!* I rear-ended the car in front of me at a busy intersection of Dupont Circle, the absolute worst place to drive a car in the entire city, much less have an accident. I stared in disbelief as the driver in the car in front of me got out to inspect the damage to his bumper, an incredulous look on his face. I closed my eyes and pressed my forehead on the steering wheel. Apparently, it had become my lot in life to never have a bad-enough day that it couldn't get just a tiny bit worse. Eventually I got out of the car to speak to the other driver.

"Hey," I said rather lamely.

He was an older gentleman, in his fifties, and I could tell he was trying to decide whether he was going to be nice about this whole thing or point out that I had rear-ended him for no good reason. Fortunately for me, he chose the former.

"Hey."

"Listen, I'm sorry about this. I, uh . . . well. You see, my wife just came out of chemo." I hadn't planned on sharing this news with a random man that I rear-ended on the street, but my mind was so full of this one thought that I would have blurted it out to a dog if it had been paying close-enough attention to me.

His face looked even more incredulous than before and then became much softer. "Breast cancer?" he asked quietly. I nodded. He looked at me and said, "My wife is a cancer survivor too. She's actually in the car with me right now." He turned away from me and went back to his car window, and then he ducked in to the car to talk to his wife. I could see them speaking, and then she turned around to look at us and waved. He came back and said very seriously, "Son, I know exactly how you feel," patting me gently on the shoulder. "You'll get through this, just like we did."

I nodded dumbly, blinking back tears.

"Don't worry about this; the damage is nothing serious. We'll let insurance hammer this all out. You guys . . . you just hang in there. Everything will be okay."

I nodded again and thanked him for his kindness. This was exactly what I had yearned for when I was in the stairwell with Carol and the girls, for someone to tell me that everything would be okay. I just didn't expect it to come from a man whom I rear-ended in the middle of rush-hour traffic. It was a powerful reminder that God hadn't forgotten about us in all of this and that he would be that bigger and stronger Father who would comfort me in my times of sorrow.

But it was also a reminder that God was committed to doing things in his own utterly incomprehensible way and time.

● ● ●

For Carol's third chemotherapy session, I was able to find someone to take care of the girls so that I could accompany her to treatment. I had never been to a chemo ward before and was surprised to discover that each patient did not have his or her own private room but instead shared a common room where they all received treatment together. Over a dozen recliners sat side by side, tangles of medical equipment between each of them. It was in these recliners that patients received treatment, usually while reading books or listening to music. The room was large and bright, surrounded by windows that provided a beautiful sweeping view of Georgetown's campus and surrounding neighborhoods.

Having always received medical care in a private room, or at least separated by a curtain, I found this arrangement a little strange and disconcerting at first. I would have always imagined that people would prefer to be by themselves during treatment. But it dawned on me that this might be done on purpose. Receiving treatment together like that forged a strange but vital sense of community. Everyone there could see one another and realize they were not alone, which I'm sure was a great comfort. Sometimes a room to ourselves is the last thing we need.

It was also interesting to see the diversity of people gathered there. Unlike the waiting rooms for breast cancer specialists, the chemotherapy room was not just composed of older women, but people of all ages and both genders. There were very old people, to be sure, but also young adults the same age as Carol, or perhaps even younger. All races were represented as well: African Americans, Caucasians, Asians. It was a clear reminder that cancer is a scourge to all humanity and leaves no group untouched.

I held Carol's hands as she sat in her recliner, waiting for her treatment to get started. When her nurse came by to start the chemotherapy, the first thing she did was pull on a thick pair of blue rubber gloves—not the thin kind that doctors and nurses use for examinations, but the thick kind that chemists use in experiments. Casually I said to her, "Wow, those are some heavy-duty gloves! Why do you use those instead of the thin latex ones?" I said this with a smile, thinking it was for some lighthearted reason, like the ward had run out of regular gloves her size.

But as she prepared the reddish fluid that was going to be injected into Carol, she explained: "I don't usually use these, but the chemicals we use for your wife's treatment are pretty caustic, and they can actually burn skin. So we have to wear these gloves to prevent that from happening."

My smile quickly faded. A chemical so caustic that it burns skin was going to be pumped directly into the veins of my wife. And as the nurse depressed the plunger that would release the chemotherapy drugs, I winced. I could not help but imagine that chemical coursing through Carol's entire body and swirling around our baby, so vulnerable and delicate inside Carol's womb. I imagined these things and had to bite my lip to keep from crying. How were both of them going to survive this process?

It was that day I truly became aware of how terrible chemotherapy is. It kills any cells that divide and proliferate quickly, which includes cancer, but many other cells as well. The doctor also told us that the chemo would destroy Carol's eggs and that she would not be able to have any more children as a result, what they termed *early menopause*. In addition, the treatments would affect her white blood cells, compromising her immune system and making it far easier for her to get sick. Her red blood cell count would also plunge, causing anemia and completely sapping her of energy. As a result, she would need periodic blood transfusions to keep her energy up.

And of course, Carol's hair began to fall out as well. I didn't notice anything at first. But eventually I started to see more and more hair around the house, when I swept the floor, or in the drain of the bathtub. Carol told me her hair had become so fragile that she could pull it out with hardly any effort, just a simple tug. I knew we had come to a crucial crossroads, and I didn't know what to say or suggest.

With all of the other side effects of chemotherapy, you could, with effort, maintain some sense of normalcy. You could wear gloves or paint your fingernails to cover their discoloration. You could wear makeup to hide the dark circles under your eyes, although my wife did neither of these things. But once you lost your hair, you passed a threshold. You could maybe choose to wear a colorful scarf or purchase a wig, but to most people, the truth would still be painfully clear—you had cancer.

I stood there quietly, waiting to hear what Carol wanted to do. Finally, she said, "Honey, can you get your clippers and shave it all off?"

"Sure," I replied. "Is that what you want to do? Because . . . you can't really go back on that choice, you know." Yes sir, Captain Obvious reporting for duty.

She paused before replying with finality, "Yes. I don't want to walk around with a few strands on my head. Just cut it all off."

I nodded and got my clippers ready. For the next hour or so, I carefully shaved all of Carol's beautiful shoulder-length hair

Carol, before and after I shaved her head.

from her head, where it fell in heaps on the floor by her feet. We hardly spoke during the process, and so the only other sound in the room was the buzzing drone of the clippers. After I was done, we looked in the mirror together and didn't say a word. A totally different woman stared back at us. Carol was bald, her scalp shiny and pale, her eyes even larger when no longer framed by her dark hair. We didn't know what to say or how we should feel in that moment. All we knew was that we had passed into a dark and unknown season of life.

● ● ●

While I spent most of this time worrying about Carol, Carol spent most of her time worrying about me. She knows I am not the most emotionally resilient person in the world, and am very prone to discouragement. It is shocking how little it takes for me to slide into depression—an innocent comment that someone makes or does not make, a wrongly perceived look given by someone who had the misfortune of looking somewhere in my general vicinity at the wrong time. Carol was concerned that the mishap-filled first service of the church and these first months of chemotherapy might initiate a season of depression for me. It had happened before, and with far less provocation.

But it didn't, not this time. Even though these events were very discouraging, and by all rights should have sent me into an emotional tailspin, they only dealt me a glancing blow. In fact, I had forgotten about many of them for years. But I cannot take any credit for this, as if it were my incredible mental fortitude that allowed me to shake off those disappointments. If anyone deserves credit for this miracle, it is my daughters.

Before she got sick, it was Carol who took care of most of the chores around the house, as well as the girls' day-to-day needs. I would try my best to help but mostly just got in the way. But once she got sick, I knew that had to change. I started doing all the chores around the house that Carol would allow me to do, which included cleaning the house, washing dishes, and doing the laundry. This last chore was no small feat, as before that time, I was genuinely intimidated by the washing machine, with all its complex buttons and its use of the term *delicates*.

I also helped to take care of our daughters in a more significant way. I would walk Sophia to school in the morning and help take care of Katie throughout the day. In the afternoon, Katie and I would pick Sophia up from school, and we would all come home and play together or watch videos until dinner. After dinner, there was a little more time for play, and then bed.

And after all of this, I would furiously work on my sermon and other church matters, all before flopping onto my bed and falling into the dreamless sleep that often accompanies utter exhaustion. But at seven each morning, my daughters would march into my room, as regular as cuckoos in a clock, and I would do it all again.

As a result, I experienced a kind of tiredness that I had never felt before, not even when Sophia and Katie were newborns—narcoleptic levels of fatigue. I began to fall asleep at random hours of the day and in incredibly random places. One time, after picking Sophia up from school, I turned on an episode of *Dora* for her but fell asleep before the last "Go, Dora, go!" of the opening credits was proclaimed. I was so deep in sleep that I didn't even wake up when Sophia, bored with her video and perhaps a little annoyed at my total lack of attentiveness, started

Exhausted dad/bored daughter.

169

Captain Katie and the USS *Dad*. That's me under the cushions, oblivious that I was made into a ship.

to draw on my face with a crayon, swooping around my eyes and cheeks. Bet you didn't know you could draw on someone's face with a crayon, but you can.

Another time, after I had fallen asleep on the couch, Katie threw pillows over me and then perched herself on top, a hand-drawn map in her hands. When asked by Carol, Katie informed her that she was pretending that she was the captain of a ship, lurching in uncertain, snoring seas. I myself have no recollection of that moment, but I know it happened because Carol managed to take a picture so that I could see for myself.

This may sound terrible, but I honestly believe that being exhausted was the best thing for me at the time. Exhaustion helped me avoid the depression that would have been otherwise inevitable, because I just didn't have the time or energy for it.

I didn't have time to think about how bad the launch of the church had gone. I didn't have the mental energy to expend on Carol's chemotherapy. I was a parent and a husband and had far too much on my plate to sit there brooding on the past. But this also meant zero energy for cynicism and zero time for brooding about the future. And zero chance of getting stuck in my own mind.

As strange and contradictory as it seems, I think peace often comes not from dwelling on things *more*, but rather, dwelling on them *less*. We usually see emotional self-indulgence as a good thing—it's good for us to vent to friends about our frustrations, and good to think about our lives and situations deeply. I think that is true, but only to an extent. If we go too far in this practice, our negativity can begin to percolate within us, and negative emotions can become sharpened, not dulled. And so I believe part of my emotional saving grace stemmed from the fact that my girls kept me too tired to be depressed.

Being busy also forced me to live in the moment, where I became more aware of daily blessings. Because Carol and I were spiritually and physically living hand to mouth, we did not have the energy to focus on anything else besides the moment that we immediately found ourselves in. It takes energy and time to think about the past and the future, and we had no energy to spare for such luxuries. So despite the questions we had about the past and the uncertainty that loomed in the future, we did not think about either very much. We were focused only on getting through that particular day, and nothing further.

With this intense daily focus came the surprising realization that every day was filled to the brim with blessings. If the girls were well-behaved on a certain day, that was no small thing to us. We knew that if they weren't and insisted on throwing fits throughout the day, our day would be tremendously difficult in turn. Often people would send dinner to us from local restaurants, and every single time they did, it was nothing less than manna from heaven. It meant we would not have to go grocery shopping as often and did not have to take the extra hour or two to prepare dinner. We could instead spend that time with one another or sleeping, two incredibly precious gifts. If traffic going to or from the hospital was good, that was a blessing. If it wasn't raining, that was a blessing. If we survived to 9 p.m. with relatively happy children, having had a relatively okay day ourselves, that was a blessing. That is the beauty of living hand to mouth—you become aware of how each day is filled with God's providence.

There is a verse in Scripture that testifies to this dynamic. In Psalm 118:24, the psalmist writes, "This is the day that Lord has made; let us rejoice and be glad in it" (ESV). This is a well-known verse to many Christians, but we often don't realize that the Hebrew word used for *day* is far more descriptive than its English counterpart. It is the Hebrew word *yom*, which is often translated as "from sunrise to sunset." That definition provides clearer chronological sense of what the psalmist is trying to communicate. In some way, it's as if the psalmist is saying, "In the span of this one day, from sunrise to sunset, there is something to rejoice and be glad in!" This was the realization that I made during that season—that each day, from sunrise to sunset, contained some small but precious sign of God's love and providence.

But there was one more way in which my daughters saved me from depression. When we first found out about Carol's cancer, one of our first and most troubling concerns was how we were going to tell the girls and how they would respond. Carol and I tried our best to explain what cancer was and what was going to happen. We wanted to strike a balance and convey the enormity of our situation without overwhelming them, to be honest but still hopeful.

But when I think back to my daughters during that time, I don't remember tantrums or night terrors or fits of anxiety, as natural as those behaviors would have been. No, I mostly remember dancing.

When Carol was receiving chemo, Beyoncé's "Single Ladies" was at the very height of its popularity. Sophia was especially taken with Beyoncé and demanded we hold nightly dance parties that featured just that one song, played on infinite repeat. And so we did. Even at four, Sophia was a graceful dancer who could imitate the moves from the "Single Ladies" video with uncanny precision, especially the syncopated downward fist pumping/knee raises featured in the song. Katie had no interest in dance moves—she wanted only to jump. She would demand that we boost her up on the sofa: "Halp? *Halp?!*" she would squawk. And once there, she would leap back down to the carpet, always sticking the landing and wearing the same manic smile on her face that she does to this day.

Carol and I were much too exhausted to dance with the same enthusiasm as Sophia and Katie. We tried our best to keep up, shuffling about tiredly, our heels rarely leaving the floor. Mostly, we just watched our daughters and smiled.

As hard as those weeks and months were on Carol and me, our daughters filled our home with laughter and joy. We baked Christmas cookies together, their cheeks stained red and green from the sugar they licked from their creations. We spent hours playing in the four-foot snowdrifts outside our house, where the girls would constantly get stuck and cry out for someone to lift them out onto cleared ground. After treatment sessions, Carol would often go to bed before the girls did, and on those days, the girls would read her a bedtime story, positively bursting with pride each time.

By the grace of God, our daughters flourished and were happy. This made both Carol and me deeply happy in turn, blunting the impact of what might have been a terribly depressing season for us both. Their joy and laughter became ours, a kind of blessing bestowed from children to parents, rather than the other way around. There is a passage in Romans 12 that testifies to this dynamic, when Paul commands us to weep with those who weep, but also to be happy with those who are happy (verse 15). What a blessing that it is not just sorrows we can share vicariously with others, but joy and happiness as well. So even in seasons where we may have little to smile or laugh about in our individual lives, we are not robbed of all reason for joy. We have the joy of others, which can become ours in turn.

I remember when I shaved Carol's hair and we were looking in the mirror together, divided as to how we should feel. Curious as to what was going on, Sophia and Katie slowly ventured into the room. They caught sight of their mother without any hair and stared wordlessly. We stared back. But then they began laughing and pointing, saying, "Look, Mommy has no hair! She looks just like Daddy now! Mommy and Daddy are both bald!" I hadn't realized it, but they were right. I regularly shaved my head and had done so not long before. So as our daughters observed, our hairstyles were not so different from one another. It was almost as if we had planned it this way, to be a matching bald couple, if that's a thing people would ever want to coordinate.

Although lighthearted, that moment was a critical one for us—to hear our daughters say something as dire as "Mommy has no hair," not with melancholy, but with unabashed hilarity. As Carol and I looked at each other, with our daughters laughing and jumping in the background, smiles came to our lips. What could have been a traumatic moment had unexpectedly turned into one of humor and real joy.

God used my daughters to teach me an important lesson and further rebuild my understanding of what life with him is really like. He taught me that deep pain and deep joy can coexist. I think I often have a very binary view toward life. Either I am happy, or I am sad. Either things are going well, or they are going badly. Either one or the other, but never both. And this dualistic perspective often causes us to miss out on so much of life. When we are doing well, we forget the open wounds we and others carry; when we suffer, we are blind to the joys that are right in front of our faces or else feel it is somehow immoral to crack a smile.

The reality is, blessing and suffering often coexist with one another. One image captured this lesson perfectly for me. In our yard, we have a small mulberry tree, which typically bears a dark-purple and very sweet berry. But I knew the tree would never bear fruit, because it was completely overtaken by a wisteria vine, which while being very pretty is also very invasive. When we moved into our house that winter, we were sure the tree was as good as dead. The wisteria was massive, encircling the tree from its roots to its branches, so entwined that it was difficult to tell the vine from the tree itself.

But as we approached summer, we noticed the tree was growing leaves and then pinkish berries that would eventually ripen to dark purple. And not just a few mulberries, but bushels worth, bending the branches with their weight. Even though the tree was encircled by that nasty vine, it was bearing fruit.

I thoughtfully regarded the tree from my living room window, and I realized that this was a perfect metaphor for my wife and her own struggle. An invasive form of breast cancer had taken hold of her, spreading its tendrils from her chest to her arm, threatening to spread and choke the life out of her. But she resisted and refused, fighting its influence and even bearing fruit.

I saw my wife in that beautiful tree and wept at the power of the image and the strength of my wife. And then I immediately took my axe and chopped that damnable wisteria to bits and burned those bits to ashes.

To learn to accept the inevitable comingling of blessing and suffering, joy and sadness, disappointment and hope is to learn how to live fully. It is to find yourself in a painful place but to also realize that the sun still rises, and small but precious blessings can be found, even in a wasteland. It is to be lonely but happy, sick but at peace, filled with joy and compassion, hopeful yet sober. Christians are often loath to adopt this mentality, believing that acknowledging human brokenness and pain somehow diminishes the victory of God. But we forget our church history and the lives of saints who suffered terribly and then praised God in the very same breath. Their anguish did not in any way diminish the power and victory of God but instead affirmed that God is present in all moments of our lives, valleys and mountaintops alike. God's presence is not confirmed through one positive moment and then invalidated by a more negative one.

He is Lord over them both—and over all.

A (Minor) Miracle

n the summer months of 2010, I inexplicably got caught up in mopeds. If you do not know what mopeds are, allow me a moment to provide a quick description: A scooter is not the same thing as a moped. A bicycle is not the same thing as a moped. A moped can be imagined either as a scooter with pedals or as a bicycle with an engine, whichever image is easier to conjure up. While not many companies make mopeds anymore, they are quite popular in the hipster community. I suppose this is because hipsters like things that look vintage and goofy, which describes mopeds quite well.

In June of that year, I purchased my first moped from Craigslist. It was made in India and barely worked, but through some gigantic stroke of luck, I was able to fix it and sell it for as much as I had paid. With that money, I bought a different moped, which I enjoyed for a while but ended up trading for another moped, and so on and so forth. Over the period of just a few years, I have bought or sold fifteen mopeds or scooters and usually made a modest profit on most of the sales. I used those profits to purchase my final dream moped: a 1977 J.C. Penney Pinto . . . that barely worked—and that I have since sold.

I enjoyed my season of moped mania on several different levels. First, if there is a better feeling than puttering through the National Arboretum in the middle of summer, every plant and flower in full bloom, I don't know what it is. Winning the Super Bowl, perhaps. Second, it's much harder to hurt yourself when you're going only twenty-five miles an hour, which is the maximum speed of the average moped, a fact that comforted my wife. But finally, I liked how girls stared at me when I rode my moped around the city . . . and guys . . . and children. Pretty much everyone on the street stared at me when I motored around on my moped, but more with confusion than admiration.

Part of the reason that mopeds gripped me with such fascination is the intense attention to detail that it requires to repair one. Mopeds have the simplest combustion engine known to man, the two-stroke engine. Gas is mixed with oxygen, then sprayed into a fine mist, where it is ignited by a spark plug. The resulting explosion creates gas and pressure, which drives a piston. Not much to it, when you describe this process in broad terms. But that's not the full story. The truth is, even though mopeds have such simple engines, there are a million things that can, and do, go wrong with them. And so in order to fix a bike that is not running, you have be intensely focused on details: Is the carburetor clean enough to eat from, assuming you would want to do something like that? Are the bolts on the engine head torqued correctly? Are the gas and air mixing in the correct ratio? Did you turn the switch from "off" to "run"? Details like that.

That sense of minute focus was just about the only thing that could take my mind off my family's situation. It became a

Working on mopeds, including my dream one here, a 1977 J.C. Penney Pinto, was a welcome distraction.

mental refuge, a place to unplug from the omnipresent reality of cancer, chemotherapy, pregnancy, and church planting. I didn't think about any of those things while working on my moped. While working on a bike, my only and all-consuming thought was this: "WHY ISN'T THIS STUPID THING RUNNING?" As infuriating as that question was, it was still infinitely preferable to the alternatives: "Will my wife, child, and church survive this year? *Will I?*" Although we tend to conceive of obsessions as negative, they are not a bad sort of thing if they allow us to stop obsessing about something else, something worse, something that could have legitimately driven us mad. Thus obsessions, like nearly all aspects of life, are to be judged relatively.

179

What is also noteworthy about this hobby was that I was able to indulge in it at all. When Carol's treatments first began, I was so physically drained there was no way that I could have enjoyed time to do anything that wasn't directly related to my family or to church. But the summer was not as sharply tumultuous as the events of the winter and spring had been. There were no more letters from the insurance company, no new frightening revelations about Carol's condition, no news that the doctors had made a mistake and that we were going to have triplets. Our lives had become less fraught and uncertain.

This allowed our family to at last find some kind of regularity, albeit of a bizarre sort. We had become accustomed to Carol's treatments, knew how much time she would need to recover after each session, and had adjusted our weekly schedule appropriately. She would have treatments on Thursday and, as a result, would feel nauseous and fatigued for the next few days. So I would step up in my daddy duties around the house, at least until the weekend passed, after which Carol would usually feel much better, almost her usual self. And on Thursday, we would do it all over again. It was nice to have a weekly rhythm, even if that rhythm involved going to the hospital so that your wife could have poisons injected into her body.

I had also become a seasoned veteran around the house and no longer had to ask Carol where the laundry detergent was, and the toilet brush, and which socks belonged to which daughter. Not that I ever truly figured that last part out—I just threw them into a pile on the girls' bedroom floor and asked them to sort it out themselves, which they never refused to do. I had finally become a competent, even confident, father and caretaker, and all it took to accomplish such a feat was my wife falling gravely ill. Honestly, given my previous incompetency, nothing less would have sufficed. That is one of the hidden benefits of suffering—its ability to change and even improve aspects of yourself that you had never been able to change before, whether you wanted to change them or not.

We even began to venture out of the house more often. I took the girls to the local pool, only one block away from where we lived. I would rarely enter the water myself, as a result of a phobia that stems from imagining everything little children do beneath the water. And so I would watch them from a pool chair and was always struck by the sight of my two Korean daughters, with their ivory skin and straight black hair, bobbing up and down among a sea of African-American children. I felt some mild apprehension about my children being so different from everyone else. But as was the case when I sent Sophia to the local school, both of my daughters were treated the same as anyone else, playing tag with the other timid children in the shallow end while desperately trying to avoid the splash wars and cannonballs of the older boys. We went there several times a week until the day a man was shot right outside the entrance of the pool, a drug deal gone bad. I promptly bought an inflatable pool for the girls instead, which I parked right outside my back door and watched like a hawk.

In July, when Carol was seven months' pregnant, we went to an amusement park called Dutch Wonderland, so called for its proximity to Pennsylvania Dutch country. There was little evidence of the Amish when we were there, except for an exhibit of Amish life in the center of the park that featured animatronic mannequins wearing traditional Amish attire. I think they were there to help educate people on the life of Christian traditionalists, but I remembered nothing from that exhibit but the soulless eyes of those robots and their jerky motions. My daughters wisely avoided that area altogether. The park rides made me feel queasy, not because of their daring speed, but because of their sheer nauseating clankiness. It took five minutes for me to realize that Dutch Wonderland was nothing more than a poor man's alternative to Disneyland, which made it absolutely perfect for my family and me.

I tried to have a good time while there but found it increasingly difficult to ignore the stares of every person we passed by, their eyes inexorably drawn to this heavily pregnant woman with a shaved head who walked by my side. They stared so long and shamelessly I swear I could almost hear their thoughts: *Why did this pregnant woman shave her head?* One woman stared so long that I lunged toward her and hissed, "IT'S CANCER." Her eyes wide with shock and her face as red as a turkey's, she scurried past us, while I shot laser beams of malice at her through my eyes. It is hard to put into words just how satisfying that moment was for me. But honestly, who can blame that woman for being unable to look away from this jarring juxtaposition, a powerful and saddening image of cursedness and blessing, of health and sickness—of life and death?

This was the kind of normalcy we had achieved in life, as normal of a life as you can have when you live in the city and are trying to plant a church, all while your wife is pregnant and going through chemotherapy—which is to say, not very normal at all. But after nine months of being in a state of nearly constant paranoid skittishness, this was much better than anything else we had experienced thus far. And so I finally allowed myself to settle down.

But I should have known better.

●　●　●

By early August, we had entered the home stretch of this exhausting and harrowing season of life. Carol had only a few more rounds of treatment to go before she was finished. Then she would have a two-week break before the baby was scheduled to be born, in mid-September. After that, she would still have to undergo radiation treatments, which had far fewer side effects compared to chemotherapy. The end, it appeared, was finally in sight.

I came into the house one afternoon from working on my most recent moped acquisition, a bike from the 1970s that had been manufactured in an Eastern European country that no longer exists. Its piston had frozen in its cylinder, so I had spent the better part of the day happily whacking it with a hammer, hoping to separate the two. I came inside in a wonderful mood, a smile on my face and my hands covered in grease, when I saw Carol sitting at the table. She looked up at me, her brow furrowed, and wearing an expression I instantly recognized—the same one she had worn while sitting at the table before finding out about the miscarriage, or when reading the letter of termination from our health insurance company. But the look that day was even worse, one of naked fear. With a querulous voice, she said, "Peter . . . I haven't felt the baby move in a few days, since the last chemotherapy treatment."

That had been Thursday. It was now Sunday, four days with no movement. Before I could say anything, she quickly added, "I know . . . I know I should have told you earlier, but I didn't want to make a big deal of it because this kind of thing happens, and I thought the baby would shift and start moving any day. But now . . . now I'm starting to get worried . . ." She trailed off at that point, not daring to finish the thought.

A nightmarish sense of déjà vu washed over me, and I was ripped back to the memory of Carol's miscarriage one year ago, convinced it was all happening again, exactly as it had before. *That's it,* I thought to myself. *The baby is gone.* The latest round of treatment must have been too much for this little child, and it had succumbed to the toxicity. This child, who had given us so much hope and purpose in a dark season, was now lost, floating lifelessly in the womb.

I wanted to say so many things in that moment, to tell her she should have told me earlier, that she always waits too long to say something until it's too late. But in the end, all that came out of my mouth was, "Let's go. Let's go to the hospital right away," which is exactly what I should have said. She nodded in agreement, and we gathered the girls and left for Georgetown.

We didn't speak a word on the way to the hospital. There wasn't a whole lot we could say in that situation, nothing that would have really helped us anyway. It would have been useless to share banalities with one another, like "I'm sure everything is okay," or anything of that sort. We knew from firsthand experience that wasn't always true, that sometimes a doctor comes into the room and starts off by saying, "I'm sorry, but . . ." We had learned that bitter truth. But in addition, I think we were silent on the ride because we were afraid. We were afraid that if we said anything or dared to express our fear that the baby had died, it would somehow instantly become true. Silence was our final refuge.

In contrast to the quiet that dominated in the car, a continuous pleading dialogue with God went on in my head. *Please, God, no,* I prayed. *Please, please, not now. This baby is all that is keeping us together. Please don't take this baby from us. Not like the last time.* As I drove, desperately fighting back my fear and apprehension, my reformed and renewed understanding of God, so much stronger than before, began to twist and buckle under the stress.

We checked Carol into Georgetown Hospital, the same hospital where she was scheduled to deliver the baby in a few weeks. Carol was taken to labor and delivery, where the nurse asked her to lie down on the examining table so that they could take an ultrasound, all of which seemed painfully familiar to me. As I sat next to Carol, holding her hand, I was overwhelmed with the memories of the many times we had sat just like this: one year ago, when our friend Joe had told us that Carol had had a miscarriage; eight months after that, clutching our hands tightly together as Dr. Griffin shared the shocking news that Carol was pregnant. How strange that we were in the same exact position again, our hopes, our joy, our peace hanging in the balance once more.

The doctor came in and began to use an ultrasound probe to try to find the baby's heartbeat. As she moved the probe around my wife's stomach, the monitor was quiet, nothing but faint static and subtle whooshes. I knew from experience what these sounds meant and clenched my teeth, my eyes locked on the ultrasound monitor, praying for something, anything, to come through the speaker. She moved to another location, and nothing but more of the same. I prepared myself for the inevitable, for the doctor to stop the examination and break the bad news to us. She moved once more, and suddenly we heard:

LUBDUB-LUBDUB-LUBDUB-LUBDUB.

The sound of a little heart pumping and beating for all its tremendous worth. The baby was alive.

Carol's face broke and she dissolved into tears. My knees buckled, and I almost fell to the floor. I exhaled for the first time since the ultrasound started, and gave thanks to God from the deepest place in my heart. The doctor turned to us, her face beaming with the same relief we ourselves felt, and exclaimed, "There it is! The baby is doing fine; heartbeat is even and strong. Must have been resting for a while." Knowing that Carol was going through chemotherapy, she added quietly, as if almost to herself, "And I'm not surprised, after all this baby has been

185

through already." We thanked the doctor profusely and looked at one another. Once more God demonstrated that he had a plan, and that plan would not fail.

When we stepped out of the hospital that afternoon, we felt relief beyond words. The oppressive summer heat engulfed us as we left the front door, but it felt good and only served to remind us that we were alive—all of us. But I didn't just feel good. I felt jubilant, deeply blessed, and loved by God. I felt like shouting into the air, shaking random people's hands, and ordering a round of drinks for everyone at a local bar. Instead, before we pulled out of the parking lot, Carol and I held hands to say a short prayer of thanksgiving: "Father God, thank you. Thank you for saving our child. Thank you for this amazing miracle."

It might seem strange to call this moment a miracle, because it does not seem to fit the classic definition for such a thing. After all, hearing that the baby was alive was something to be very happy about—surely a relief, but not really a miracle. A miracle would have been if the baby had turned his or her face to the screen and given a thumbs-up, indicating everything was perfectly fine. THAT would have qualified as a miracle. But to simply hear the baby's heartbeat and discover he or she was still alive—that's just good news, not to mention the fact that the baby had not yet been born and Carol's cancer not yet eliminated, which made any jubilation premature in many ways.

But I contend that moment was indeed a miracle, because I knew from firsthand experience what the news might have been. I fully expected the doctor to turn to tell us that she was unable to find a heartbeat, and the baby was dead. Experiences at the church had further impressed this heartbreaking truth upon me. Riverside families had seen a few babies born, but nearly all of them came with frightening complications. One pregnancy was followed by a severe bout with postpartum depression, and in another, the child did not make it safely into his parents' arms, only into the arms of his heavenly Father. I had the terrible responsibility and honor of committing that tiny baby into the hands of God. Having seen all of these things firsthand, I knew for a fact that finding out a baby is alive and healthy is not unremarkable news. Hearing that powerful pulsing sound of a healthy heart was nothing short of a miracle worth celebrating, a cause to shout in joy and relief.

These experiences have made me think about God, and the nature of miracles in general. Perhaps the reason we in the modern world have such a difficult time perceiving miracles is the fact that our lives are so idiotically pleasant already. Our definition of a miracle implicitly becomes a great blessing we experience in addition to the great blessings that we have come to expect every day. We already have good jobs, health, friends, relationships, love, and joy and very rarely experience true life-threatening hardship. And so miracles are something like icing on a cake, a bit of sweetness layered on top of a cake that already has several cups of sugar baked into it. And in that context, a miracle has to be truly supernatural and crazy for us even to become aware of it. If it is not, it becomes mundane, lost amidst all the other blessings that surround our lives. It's like trying to see the stars shining in the middle of the day when the sun is out and there is not a cloud in the sky.

The mysterious blessing of suffering is that it provides the starkest of backdrops against which we become acutely aware of the miracles that surround us. Such was the case in the early church from the book of Acts. We tend to focus on the fact that the period of the early church was filled with miracles, and we pray for such things to take place in our midst as well. But we often forget the church also witnessed terrible violence daily. Believers in the early church were fed to lions, lit on fire to light the Colosseum, or boiled in brass pots. Their everyday reality was one completely opposite of our own. We forget that the disciples, as miracle-filled as their lives were, were nearly all martyred for following Jesus. That is the context of the book of Acts—abundant miracles, but set in juxtaposition with suffering.

Miracles were easy for the church to identify because they contrasted so much with their dominant reality. They would rejoice when people were released from jail after being whipped and tortured because they knew firsthand that often people were never seen again, or seen in bloody pieces. I hardly think many of us would consider such a thing a "miracle" in our age.

So I believe that God is still a God of miracles, as active as he has always been. The reason we cannot discern his divine providence is that we do not lack for anything. After all, what does providence mean to a person who has it all? How would you be able to see the mighty protection of God unless you were first under attack? And how can someone be saved unless they know they are dying first? No, it is suffering that allows us to see God's blessings most clearly and miracles more regularly. No wonder reports of miracles are common in parts of the world where the church faces regular persecution—in China, Africa, and the Middle East—and so rare here in the West, where persecution is equally rare.

That night, after we had returned from Georgetown, I had a hard time falling asleep. It was partially due to the adrenaline that had been pumping through me for the past few hours, and that my emotions refused to disembark from the dizzying roller coaster they had been forced to ride all afternoon. It was exhausting to experience such a wide range of emotions in such a short period, but unfortunately, it was that irrational kind of "exhausting" that does nothing but keep you awake all night.

Of course, Carol had no such problems and was sound asleep, snoring softly.

As I lay there, I realized the experiences of that single day in many ways mirrored those of my entire year. I had never suffered so much in my entire life as I had in the past year. It was as if a decade's worth of arduous experiences had been compressed into an impossibly small time frame. And in that time, I had experienced depths of fear and doubt unlike anything ever before.

But before I could become too discouraged by this fact, I realized something else, something even more wonderful: Never before had I witnessed God so clearly at work as I had in the past year. Sure, I had seen God work in big and small ways before then. God had been present in my life, but it was hazy, as if it was difficult to discern his handiwork from the good things that already filled my life. I would often thank God for this or that, as all good Christians do, but I would simultaneously wonder if it was truly God alone who had provided those blessings or if it was my education, my upbringing, or pure dumb luck.

But this year was different. The reality of God's presence and his plan was stark and concrete, defying misattribution of any kind. One conversation I had earlier in the spring captured this perfectly: Toward the end of Sophia's school year, I was picking her up from school when her teacher, Mrs. Stevens, asked how my wife was doing. Mrs. Stevens knew Carol had cancer, but not much more than that. So I tried to summarize everything that had happened since the diagnosis, a nearly impossible feat—the debacle with the insurance, finding out about her pregnancy, and our difficult decision to keep the baby. With every twist and turn of our story, Mrs. Stevens's eyes widened, and she would occasionally gasp and hold her hands to her mouth. I concluded by saying, "And after all that, Carol is actually doing pretty well.

She's getting through treatment, and the baby is healthy and actually will be born in just a couple of months!"

Many people to whom I told our story would blandly respond with, "Wow, that's incredible! You guys are so lucky!" or some other expression of generic thanksgiving. But Mrs. Stevens's eyes narrowed, and she looked about the room at her co-teacher and the other parents in the room who had heard our conversation. Then, raising both arms to the ceiling and pointing each index finger as far as they would extend, she proclaimed at the top of her voice, "That's God! That's GOD!" to which everyone else in the room nodded vigorously in affirmation, followed by a hearty chorus of amens.

That was the kind of year we had had—a "That's God!" kind of year.

And it was no accident that these two seasons coincided with one another—one of intense suffering in life and the other of a newfound awareness of God. The painful events of the past year provided a terrible and desolate backdrop against which I could unmistakably distinguish the power and presence of God. It was like looking up into the darkest night sky and only then realizing you never knew stars could shine so brightly.

12

Nothing Can Hinder the Lord From Saving

Finally, September of 2010. Fourteen months since our miscarriage. One year since we purchased our home, only to discover it had been ransacked before we even stepped through the door. Ten months since we found out Carol had breast cancer and our insurance company selected her for rescission. Nine months since I was told the truth about triple negative breast cancer, that killer of young women. Eight months since Dr. Griffin asked us that curious but wonderful question, "You are going to have this child, right?" Seven months since my phone conversation with the oncologist while walking in the Sculpture Garden of the National Mall. Six months since the disastrous launch of our church and the start of chemotherapy. And one month since an ultrasound revealed that our baby was not gone, just having a well-deserved rest.

A period of a little over one year, filled with intense trials and hardships, more than we had experienced in all the previous years of our lives combined. And it would all come down to this month and the birth of this baby.

. . . *Oh no, the baby!* We hadn't gotten *anything* ready for the baby.

Between church planting, chemotherapy treatments, and taking care of our daughters, Carol and I were a bit too preoccupied to put together your stereotypical baby's room. You know the kind that I'm talking about: a room painted some nauseating shade of pastel, featuring giant letter blocks that spelled out the baby's name, and of course a giant stuffed animal hunched pathetically in a corner. In other words, a scene ripped straight from the pages of the latest Pottery Barn Kids catalog.

Even if we had had the time to paint the baby's room (we didn't), we wouldn't have known whether to paint it blue or pink, because we didn't know if the baby was a boy or a girl. We had done this on purpose, thinking it would be quite exciting to discover the baby's gender right as the baby was being delivered, as if our lives didn't contain enough excitement already. Likewise, even if we had had the time to go to Pottery Barn and pick out oversized letter blocks (we didn't), we wouldn't have known which letters to select because we hadn't decided on the baby's name.

Not that my opinion on the matter counted for much anyway, as all of my suggestions for baby names had been consistently shot down over the years. I had wanted to name our first daughter Jocelyn and our second, Michaela. Carol never outright refused either of these suggestions, but instead she would quietly change the conversation whenever I brought it up, which is her way of putting her foot down. And so we went with her choices and named our daughters Sophia and Kathryn, which happen to be two of the most widely used girls' names of the past decade. My daughters are destined to grow up constantly hearing their names called by people, only to realize they are really addressing some other girl named "Sofia" or "Katherine." And it will all be my wife's fault . . . although most everything else that my daughters endure will probably be mine.

But these are not the real reasons we hadn't found out about the baby's gender or decided on a name. The truth was, neither of these things mattered to us—not really. This child had already been through so much to get to this point, swimming in a toxic cocktail of drugs that had been designed to help his or her mother fight cancer, not to be safe for fragile unborn children. So boy or girl, named Abednego or Apple Cinnamon, the only thing important to us was that the baby was born healthy, with ten fingers and ten toes. That was all we needed.

That, and a Korean grandmother.

Korean mothers are strange creatures. When their children have children of their own, they transform themselves from small and demure women from a tiny distant country into powerhouses of home care. They cook Korean food in vast, vast quantities—quantities more fit for chow at an army base camp than a small home—and in far better quality. They constantly do laundry. Even if something has been worn only half a day and you took it off because the day was warmer than you expected—*bam*—it's in the machine before you can put it back on. Everything gets folded promptly; even underwear gets ironed. Children get babysat for free. For parents expecting a child, it's a dream come true.

So we knew our very first priority—before baby clothes, before a baby crib, even before a name—was to make sure that either my mom or Carol's mom would be present when the baby was born. That way we could just leave for the hospital, confident the girls would be well cared for and fed all the Korean food they could eat. But the trick was trying to decide when we should fly Carol's mom into town. If she came too late, we would have to find other friends to look after the girls when labor started, no small task in a city full of single working adults. But even worse was if she flew in too early, because her Korean grandmother superpowers would go to waste, and there was even the chance she might have to leave before the baby was born. In the end, we made an arbitrary decision to fly her in on the night of September 8, as that seemed just as good of a day as any other. We just hoped it would be close enough to the actual day that the baby was born.

With that first and most important decision out of the way, we made things ready the best we could. I put together the old crib, the same one Sophia and Katie had slept in, and a good friend of ours let us borrow baby clothes they had been meaning to give away. The only things missing were baby linens and blankets, which after her miscarriage the previous year, Carol had given to charity. We considered buying a whole new set of each for the baby, but in the end, we opted to save a few bucks by making use of the blankets and towels we already had at hand. After all, the baby would hardly be able to tell the difference between baby blankets and regular ones, at least not until he or she was older and realized from baby pictures that all the other children in the family had been swaddled in fancy embroidered blankets, and not in a Strawberry Shortcake beach towel.

Finally, September 8 rolled around, the day Carol's mom was scheduled to arrive from Seattle. Carol hadn't gone into labor, which was good. But at the same time, labor didn't seem imminent either. This worried us, because it was possible that the baby might come later, maybe even after Carol's mom left for home again. But there was no sense in worrying about something we had no control over. All we could do was hope and pray the baby would arrive soon.

I picked up Carol's mom from Reagan Airport at around ten that night. As I got out of the car to grab her suitcase and open the passenger side door for her, I was reminded of how Carol is the spitting image of her mother, both in appearance and character. She is a strikingly beautiful and gracious woman, with the same quiet strength about her as my wife. She also has the same tendency to keep things bottled up for far too long in order to spare people any inconvenience.

For instance, the day Carol and I were married, Carol's mom took part in the ceremony and all the festivities late into the night, even rocking out at the dance party that took place at the end of the reception. And after all that fun, she promptly checked herself into the hospital, where doctors informed her that her appendix had burst at some point during the course of the day. She would actually have to have part of her colon removed. Afterward, while lying on the hospital bed, doubled up in intense pain, she explained to Carol that she hadn't gone to the hospital earlier because she didn't want to ruin our special day.

See? Like mother, like daughter.

As it was already late at night, and figuring that she was tired from her transcontinental flight, we promptly settled Carol's mom into her room and said good-night. We ourselves went to bed not long afterward. But a few hours later, at 3 a.m., Carol rolled over and shook me by the shoulder, something that I was not at all happy about. In my stupor, I could not comprehend why my heavily pregnant wife had to wake me up at such an ungodly hour.

"What is it?" I muttered.

"Peter, I'm having contractions."

"What?"

"I'm having contractions."

"Real ones?"

"Yes, REAL ONES. Peter, we need to go to the hospital—now!"

As it finally dawned on my sleep-addled brain that Carol was going to have the baby, I jumped out of bed and started getting ready to go, throwing on clothes and putting a few last-minute items into the bag we had prepared for labor. As I opened the passenger side door for Carol, suitcase in hand, I began to experience the most curious sense of déjà vu. Hadn't I done something very similar not too long ago? And then it hit me—I had just done the same exact thing with Carol's mom. The timing was absurdly perfect. We had chosen the time and date of Carol's mother's flight at random, simply because it seemed as good as any other and was relatively cheap. And yet here we were, able to just pack up and leave for the hospital without worrying about Sophia and Katie, as they had their grandmother there to take care of them while we were gone. As we left for the hospital, Carol's mom furiously waved from the porch. We were deeply thankful for this peace of mind and knew whom we had to thank: God. No one else could have orchestrated things so perfectly.

And for what felt like the hundredth time that year, we drove together to Georgetown Hospital, but under such starkly different circumstances from previous months. We were not going there to speak with an oncologist about our options or for Carol's chemotherapy treatments. This time we were just going as a happy couple, on their way to have a baby.

● ● ●

As we sat together in her room in the delivery ward, a doctor came and made sure Carol was doing well and looked over her chart. She looked it over and then remarked, "And I see here that you want to have this baby naturally, without an epidural," and my wife nodded in confirmation. But from my corner chair, out of Carol's field of view, I shook my head sadly and thought to myself, *Oh boy, here we go again.*

My wife had always wanted to have a child naturally, meaning without the anesthetic that women typically receive in hospitals. She had tried to do this with Sophia and Katie, but the pain had been too much for her, and she had received anesthesia at the last minute. Her desire to have a child naturally stemmed from an experience overseas where she saw women giving birth without the benefit of epidurals, laboring without a sound. She realized there is an incredible inborn strength that all women possess, herself included. And so she saw having a baby naturally as a way to push herself, both physically and mentally, like running a marathon. I asked her why she didn't just do an actual marathon instead, and she replied it was because her knees were bad. That seemed like a cop-out, so I pressed her further.

"Sweetheart . . ." I searched for the right words, not wanting to make it seem like I was against this decision, which I very much was. "You know you have nothing to prove to anyone, right? You just went through chemotherapy while pregnant. No one is going to doubt your fortitude or ability to endure. You know that, right?"

"I know that," she replied thoughtfully. "I just . . . I want to prove it to myself that I am strong enough."

Now, if you haven't picked up on this painfully obvious fact yet, my wife might be a superhero. No, she is not a flashy type of individual, so people often wrongly assume that her demure appearance means that she is timid or even weak. To be sure, my wife is quiet, sometimes disarmingly so. But as the old saying goes, "Quiet waters run deep." Carol possesses a reservoir of inner strength I have never seen the equal of—ever. For the past year, she had shouldered her difficult circumstances with such fortitude and equanimity that aside from being heavily

197

pregnant and bald, you would have never guessed what was truly going on in her life. She may be small in stature, but in spirit and in my eyes, she is nothing less than a titan, a warrior, and my personal hero. So even though I had my doubts about her going through labor without an epidural, I myself committed to helping her get through this.

After Carol had experienced mild labor pains for an hour or so, the doctor came back to check on her. When she was done, she stood up and announced, "Good news! You are progressing quite well. I'd guess we should have this baby out within the hour, I would think." We were shocked and incredibly relieved—labor was so easy this time around! We had been there for only an hour, Carol was experiencing nothing more severe than mild cramps, and now we were almost done! We both thanked God this experience would be far easier than it had been the previous two times.

Fast-forward four hours.

In that time, Carol's labor had barely progressed at all, but the pain had. She was writhing on the bed, trying to find some position that didn't hurt—maybe this arm here, maybe this leg over the side of the gurney, but there was no relief to be found. She was in agony, which she channeled by squeezing my left hand with all her might. I wear my wedding ring on my left hand, and so it is quite painful when someone squeezes it firmly, kind of like when someone plays that old schoolyard game of Mercy with you. But Carol wasn't just squeezing my hand—she was crushing it, cruelly bending my fingers around a circle of metal that was supposed to represent my wife's unending love for me.

She had finally reached the breaking point, what people call "the wall," which I guess is short for "the wall of unmitigated agony." Sweating profusely and eyes clenched shut, she breathlessly told me, "I can't do this." She followed that by saying,

"I-can't-do-this-I-can't-do-this-I-can't-do-this," only pausing long enough to take the briefest intakes of breaths between each phrase. The previous times she had hit this point, we had decided it wasn't possible to continue and so elected to take the epidural. But I remembered how important this was to her, to prove to herself that she could endure labor without drugs. So I channeled my old tennis coach and said to her, "Look, you wanted to do this. You've always wanted to do this. That's what you told me. So it's too late now; you're going to have the baby this way. Sorry."

Yes, that was the "encouragement" I gave to my wife in the last stages of labor: *Sorry, too late.* But sometimes, in situations like giving birth naturally, I think it's okay to channel some more primal and blunt sources of encouragement, the type like God had given me in the dark night of my soul so many months ago. At first, Carol didn't respond at all to my rather brusque encouragement but breathed hard for a few moments. At last, she replied, "Okay, okay, okay, okay," all while lovingly squeezing my hand as I grimaced in pain.

And so it went for another hour, wave after wave of intense pain, paired with hand squashing. But finally, early in the morning on September 9, 2010, the moment had come. The doctor urged Carol through a series of pushes, and then, with one final push from Carol, the doctor caught our child.

Our newborn son.

I watched him as he squirmed in the doctor's firm grip, tears welling in my eyes—our son, our precious son. He was quiet at first, so quiet it frightened me. But then he began to wail mightily, the volume of his cries building with every breath he took, the cry of a child who had endured and survived. The doctor quickly wrapped him in a blanket and softly laid him on my wife's chest. We stared at that boy, our son, and wept.

Ten fingers, ten toes. A fully formed body with no defects. A handsome face and a mouth as red as a strawberry. He was perfectly healthy. He had survived in his mother's womb during chemotherapy and had emerged unscathed. He was our miracle, a miracle that had almost never been.

Before long, the nurses came to pry him out of Carol's arms, and she reluctantly let him go. Desperate to keep my eyes on him, I followed the nurses to their examination table, trying to peek in between their arms and elbows to catch a glimpse of my son. He submitted to the various indignities they subjected him to: ointment spread over his eyes, his tiny legs extended so they could measure his height.

After taking all the necessary measurements, they handed him back to my wife and gave us the report: 6 pounds, 11 ounces, 21 inches long, and as far as they could tell from their initial checkup, completely healthy. As the nurse relayed this information, I shook my head in disbelief and looked at my wife, whose amazement was clear even in the midst of her exhaustion. For months, we had lived in fear of the baby being born with a severe defect or sickly and underweight. And instead, he ended up being as healthy as both of his sisters and heavier and longer than either of them!

But my son was in no mood to marvel with his father. All the fuss of the examination had put him in a foul temper, and he was on the verge of crying in that inimitable way that newborns do, his mouth open wide and eyes clenched shut. But before he could, I instinctively slid my pinky into his open mouth, and he immediately began to suckle at it. Even though this was our third child, I still marveled at how such a tiny and helpless thing could pull at my finger so strongly. He was probably thinking to himself, *This will do for now, but pretty soon I'm going to need you to hand me over to Mom.*

As he happily sucked away at my finger, I could not help but feel that even though he had been born just minutes earlier, I *knew* this boy. I felt as if I had known him for months, like he had been with us nearly every moment over the past season. And in no small way, he had. After all, he had been with us in the surgical ward with Dr. Griffin and had survived the mastectomy that followed. He was with Carol for every single chemo treatment and, more than that, endured those treatments himself. From the moment he was born, he had already experienced a lifetime of struggle, a fighter and a survivor from his very first breath.

If it had not been for this boy and his growing presence in our lives, I'm not sure my wife and I would have made it through the past year. He had given us a rare and precious gift: something to look forward to. At the end of chemotherapy, we weren't just going to pick up our lives where we had left off, as if the past year had just been some nightmarish waste of time, a black hole we hoped to leave behind. No, we were going to welcome a child into the world, a bright and beautiful light at the end of a very dark tunnel, a thought that sustained and encouraged us through it all. It was my son who transformed our struggle into a story.

That is the beauty and power of story, the sense of larger perspective and direction that it provides. Trials viewed in isolation seem to have no purpose or meaning and exist solely to make us miserable. But if we can frame our suffering into a larger story or narrative, where we can discern that suffering has not just a beginning but an end, and not just a cause but a result, we are in a far better place to make sense of the storms we face in life and journey through them to whatever lies beyond. What better example of this is there than the act of childbirth itself—hours of pain that could easily be characterized as torture, and yet women willingly endure it, as Carol did—why? *Because of the ending*, that baby, who gives purpose to the pain and even eclipses it. A painful chapter is infinitely more bearable if you know for certain that a better ending is to come. Such was the case even for Jesus himself. It was not simply raw physical and emotional fortitude combined with a Son's obedience that made it possible for Jesus to endure the various trials of his life that culminated in the violence of Good Friday. Hebrews 12:2 tells us that it was for the *joy set before him* that Jesus endured the cross, meaning that in some way, it was the shining victory that was to come that enabled Jesus to endure suffering. His endurance lay rooted in the conviction that his trials were not an end, but only the temporary means to a much greater purpose and only a chapter in the grand and glorious story of redemption.

It was with these deep thoughts that we rested in our hospital room that afternoon, our minds and hearts too full to say anything that came close to capturing how we really felt. But we did have to decide on something that day, and that was a name. What would we call our son? What name would be appropriate for this child, the manner in which we found out about him, and what he meant to our family? At first, I wanted to call him Lucas, which means "light." I thought that would be appropriate because his birth had come to us during such a hopeless time, like a bright star in the darkest night. But then I realized that kids might call him "Pukas," so I rejected the idea. But a new name came to me almost instantly.

"Let's call him Jonathan," I said. Carol looked to me, as if for an explanation.

"In Hebrew, Jonathan means 'gift of God.' I can't think of a more appropriate name for a child who was given to us at the very lowest moment of our entire lives." Carol looked thoughtfully

No caption necessary!

at the baby, considering my suggestion. Desperate to seal the deal, I continued.

"The name Jonathan also reminds me of that verse in the Bible, when Jonathan goes to battle against overwhelming odds and he says, 'Nothing can hinder the Lord from saving, whether by many or by few.' This baby is a living testimony to that."

At this, Carol smiled and nodded, then softly whispered, "Jonathan. Hello, Jonathan."

●   ●   ●

While resting in Carol's room for the next few hours, I thought back to the past year and all we had endured. To be honest, I had not been expecting much. As a Christian and a pastor, I had always espoused the infinite wisdom and power of God, as described in myriad ways in the pages of Scripture. And yet, despite this, no small part of me doubted that God could truly save us from our circumstances. They were simply too terrible and too dark to be fixed or redeemed to some greater purpose. At the beginning of this journey, over a year ago, the most I had hoped for was survival, that my wife, family, and the church would survive. Perhaps we would one day be able to make sense of our terrible situation . . . one day. But I did not expect much more than that, to survive and, perhaps one day, to forget.

We did indeed survive, which was no small blessing in itself. But in truth, we did much more than survive—we thrived. I went through the list in my head. Carol had been diagnosed with a terribly aggressive form of breast cancer, and yet here she was, sleeping next to me, as healthy as we could possibly have hoped for. And more than that even, she was strong enough to bear a child without an epidural, which requires strength on a totally different level. God had healed her and, even more, strengthened and protected her.

I thought about the tiny infant who lay sleeping in my arms and the physical environment in which he was conceived and developed. He was conceived when his mother had cancer, sharing space with a terrible invader that wanted to grow quickly, just as he did. At only ten weeks of development, Jonathan went through major surgery with his mother, powerful anesthetics coursing through both of them, her body cut open and the invader cut out. At only three months, my son would accompany his mother into chemotherapy every week or every other week, as drugs were pumped throughout her body to chase down any remaining cancer cells, drugs so caustic the nurse who administered them wore heavy rubber gloves so that her hands would not be burned by accident. And yet, after all that, here he was, perfectly healthy and whole, bigger than either of his sisters had been, no problems that anyone could identify. God had saved him so completely from the most overwhelming of hardships.

I thought about my ministry at the church. Because of Carol's diagnosis and the shaky launch of the church, it seemed we were doomed to a purposeless and unproductive ministry. But that was not the case. Because of our story, our church was able to minister more effectively to hurting people—people like Meg and many others—people who felt out of place and out of touch with bright, shiny, and well-produced churches. People came to Christ, either for the first time or after many years of running away. The gospel was preached, and prayers for healing and revival and mercy were prayed, which is what the best churches are supposed to do, no matter their size. God had forged us into a better church, and me into a better pastor.

Cradling Jonathan in the crook of my arm, I sat in the armchair of that hospital room and marveled at the truth I had witnessed over the past year—that truly nothing, not even the terrible intersection of cancer with church planting and pregnancy, could hinder the Lord from saving us.

But perhaps all of this should not have been a revelation to me. After all, what is this but the story of Jesus and the cross? The cross was historically an instrument of horror, a method of execution designed to strike the deepest fear into anyone who contemplated resisting the power of the Roman Empire. The cross proclaimed, "Resist us, and you will be nailed to this tree and set upon the side of the road for people to look at you with disgust and terror, for your enemies to mock and ridicule your nakedness and defeat. You will die slowly, suffocating as your body struggles to breathe, as blood sluggishly tries to course through your body. I dare you to resist us." That is what the cross proclaimed to all who saw it.

That is, before Jesus came.

Jesus came, and he took that challenge. He resisted the powers of this world and the world beyond in order to shatter the shackles of sin and death, and he allowed himself to be hung on that tree. And his blood forever changed the cross from a symbol of death into a symbol of something completely different. Now the cross no longer symbolizes death, but life. The ignorant and superstitious wear this execution device around their necks to ward off evil and to invite blessing—a good luck charm. In China, North Korean refugees who have fled the brutality of their country are given one piece of advice: to head for the crosses, because it is at the places that have crosses—the churches—that they will find food, rest, and support. The cross has become a symbol of freedom, for the refugee, for the slave.

And the cross that many of us see and hang up in our homes—that terrible tool of intimidation and torture—is empty. There is no body on that tree because Christ is no longer there. He died, yes, but then rose again and was seen by many. So the empty cross is a reminder of the empty tomb, that Jesus is alive. The cross has become a symbol of new life.

I could not help but cry as this truth dawned on me. Nothing could hinder the Lord from saving.

No circumstances are too dark for him to shed light upon, nothing so broken that it is beyond his ability to mend and make better. Not cancer, not hardship, not death, not even the cross—these were all as nothing before the power of his ability to save. Suffering is terrible, but it cannot bind Christ. It does not blot out his existence or curtail his power. It cannot exclude God or stop him or minimize him or move him in any way. Yes, there is suffering in life—that is true. But there is also a God whose love, blessings, and power are greater than the suffering we experience.

Holding my healthy son, sitting next to my healthy sleeping wife, I was overwhelmed by these revelations. But I had only a few more moments to digest them, as I had to leave this peaceful scene to go somewhere I really didn't want to go—to work.

Not Just Higher—*Better*

I am an in-demand speaker at many college campuses in Washington, D.C. "In demand" means that someone asked me at least once, which technically is true. And by "many," I really mean "a few," or to be even more precise . . . three. One of those three was InterVarsity Christian Fellowship at Georgetown, whose staff member e-mailed me in the spring of 2010 to see if I would speak at their weekly gathering in the coming fall. I knew Carol's delivery date was somewhere in that general time frame but figured the chances that Carol would have the baby on that exact same day were slim. After all, neither Sophia nor Katie had been born on their predicted due dates. So I agreed to speak for them, although I did inform them that there would be the smallest chance I might not be able to attend.

Of course, Jonathan decided to make his appearance the very same day I was scheduled to speak at InterVarsity. This left me in a quandary. Should I tell them I was unable to make it because my wife had just given birth to our son? That was totally justifiable, and I was certain the InterVarsity coordinator and the students would be more than understanding, given the circumstances. Yes, that was the most sensible course of action. And so as I sat in the hospital room with Carol and Jonathan, I prepared to give the coordinator a call to inform her I would not be able to make it that night.

But I just couldn't bring myself to do it. You see, I am a Korean-American pastor, and the Korean approach to ministry (and really to work of any kind) can be summarized by the following expression: "Unless you're dead, you should be working." This might sound like an exaggeration, but for those of you who know a Korean pastor, especially one who emigrated here directly from South Korea, you know this is a statement of fact.

So even though I had been up all night and my wife had just given birth to my son only a few hours ago, I decided I had to suck it up and make it to that speaking engagement. Psychotic, right? But truthfully, I had prepared the sermon months ahead of time, and the location was literally only a few blocks away. I could share my sermon and then be back with my family within two hours. Thus was my Korean pastor's guilt adequately assuaged, and I kissed my wife and newborn son and headed out to the campus.

My walk through Georgetown that afternoon was singular. I walked about in a daze, not simply because of the miracle I had witnessed just hours before, but also because it was a particularly stunning autumn day in D.C. The dusk sky was painted with rich hues of tangerine and violet, streaked with stratus clouds whose outlines glowed silver in the setting sun. The sky itself was like an enormous canvas that spanned the breadth of the entire horizon, the scope and richness of which artists since time immemorial have aspired to imitate. Trees crowned with autumn leaves framed the bottom of this canvas, the red and yellow leaves of maples and oaks broken only by the towering silhouettes of the gothic spires of Healy Hall. I smiled, imagining that some small part of the beauty was on display for my son, as if God himself were celebrating Jonathan's safe delivery.

I tried to draw my brief walk out as long as I could, but the room where they were meeting was only a quarter of a mile from the hospital, and I could pass by the entrance only so many times. So casting one final longing look at the sublime sunset, I went inside. The meeting took place in a very different environment, your typical college common room: a squarish and utilitarian space lit by fluorescent lights that flickered in the most aggravating manner. Considering how much these undergraduates paid in tuition every year, they really deserved something nicer. There were about fifty students assembled that night, none of whom I recognized. Most of the students I had personally mentored had graduated and moved on years before, so I was disappointed to discover that I could not find a familiar face.

I don't feel comfortable preaching to groups where I don't know anyone. The idea of telling a group of strangers how they should understand God and his words and how to live their lives seems bizarre to me. To combat my growing nervousness, I did what I always do in these situations, which is to lower my expectations. *No need to knock anyone's socks off or anything,* I told myself. *Just stick to what you have prepared, get this sermon done, and go back to the hospital room—easy as that.*

I settled into my front row seat, as far away from everyone as was possible in such a small space. But as I sat and reflected, a thought crossed my mind.

Maybe it is no accident that I am here.

I had been thinking about this speaking engagement as nothing more than a strange and random coincidence, that I just happened to be on campus because of Jonathan's birth. And that was my sole motivation—because I was already there, I might as well come and speak, nothing more. But after everything I had just seen and experienced, how could that possibly be the case? Was there really any such thing as a strange and random coincidence in light of a God who planned all my steps? I mean, how providential that I was slated to speak on the very same day I experienced something as amazing and life-changing as the birth of my son. And hadn't I just walked through campus in a daze, in awe of the Master Artist who wielded the world itself as his canvas? Weren't these students who were gathered here nothing less than the next generation of leaders for the church, who found themselves in a powerfully formative but fragile stage of their spiritual journeys?

And then it hit me: Nothing that had happened in the last day was an accident. It was no accident that Carol's mom had arrived hours before labor—God had planned that. And it was no accident that I found myself on campus hours before my speaking engagement with InterVarsity. God had planned that as well. He wanted me to be there and had arranged it so I would be near campus and the timing would work itself out just right. In fact, if the meeting had been a day earlier, I would not have been able to attend, because Carol would have been right in the midst of labor. Had it been a day later, I would have been busy driving Carol and our son home. This was no random occurrence, but a divinely orchestrated moment. And I realized that I needed to change my heart, my mind, and my sermon as a result.

For the first half of my talk, I stayed close to the manuscript I had prepared. I talked about the context of the book of James, how the early church in Jerusalem had undergone very real hardship and persecution: arrest, imprisonment, torture, and execution. And because of this, what they needed most was not fluffy and palatable consolations or witty aphorisms about how when God closes a door, he always opens a window. No, they required real and gritty answers, which is exactly what James provides throughout his epistle. This helps explain the startlingly frank tone that James uses, a tone that doesn't sit well with us and our placid view of life and church.

But toward the middle of the sermon, I began to instead share my testimony from the past year. I talked frankly with them about the excitement of the church plant and the disappointment of our launch. I shared how I felt betrayed by God when Carol was diagnosed and when her insurance was revoked. To the best of my ability, I tried to communicate the shock of finding out about my son in the operating room and then the long and terrible path through chemotherapy.

I concluded my testimony by saying, "You probably are wondering how this story all turns out, what happened to my wife and the baby and all that. Well, I'm happy to tell you that earlier today, not more than a few hours ago and only a couple of blocks away in the hospital on campus, my wife gave birth to a healthy son who has no complications at all—completely healthy."

A collective gasp shot through the room, followed by a spontaneous cheer that erupted from the throat of every person in attendance. It was not the kind of response I was used to receiving when I preached, but more of the kind of thing you might hear after witnessing a jaw-dropping play during a basketball or football game, when something amazing compels you to stand up and shout with joy. It was the type of response you hear when something truly great has taken place. And it was at that moment that the reality finally and fully hit me—*something truly great* had *taken place*. I had been an unwitting and often unwilling witness of and participant in a convoluted, amazing, and mysterious miracle. God had walked with my family and me through the valley of the shadow of death, and we had emerged not just unscathed, but more richly blessed than before. Everything had been planned and ordered from beginning to end, from the largest event to the smallest detail. I had seen the Master Artist paint a masterpiece upon the canvas of my own life.

God's Spirit was so clearly present in the room and in each one of our hearts. And prompted by that Spirit, I concluded, "That's my story. God is real—absolutely real. But we should be careful never to confuse reality with simplicity. God's ways are not our own, and they defy comprehension. But just because we don't understand what God is doing doesn't mean he's not up to something. His fingerprints can be seen in unique and powerful moments of our lives, and I suspect that even as I share this, some of you know exactly what I'm talking about. And if you know this is true, that God is at work in your life but you've never responded to that work before, I want you to raise your hand today and answer this God who has been pursuing you and calling you by name."

And the second I finished that last word, a young woman's hand shot up with such quickness and force, it was as if someone behind her had grabbed it and thrust it into the air, which is perhaps not too far from the truth. *So this is why God called me to this meeting*, I thought to myself—*for that young woman.* I was overjoyed and was able to then lead her in prayer as she accepted Christ as her Lord and Savior.

It was the second miraculous birth I was privileged to witness that day.

●　●　●

A few weeks later, we were a tired but healthy family of five. It was late September, and Sophia would soon be celebrating her fifth birthday and Katie her third. I would love to say that

Jonathan was doing something amazing at the time, but in the manner of all three-week-old babies, he mostly slept and ate and not much else. And as I had predicted earlier, we never got the chance to pick up proper baby supplies, so we swaddled the poor boy in a relatively soft bath towel. But it didn't matter. If he slept, to me it was a miraculous kind of sleep. If he ate, I watched him with unblinking awe. He was my amazing miracle boy. But I was not as enthusiastic about the other, rather more disgusting things he regularly did.

Carol went back into treatment, but of a different sort. She began daily radiation treatments, where doctors used powerful X rays to pinpoint different sections of her chest wall, irradiating

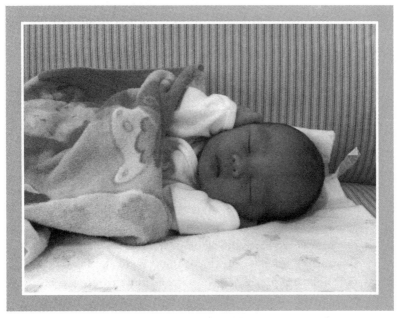

When you don't have time to shop for baby supplies, a Strawberry Shortcake beach towel will do (September 2010).

the flesh so that no new cancers could develop there. This sounds brutal, but the treatment was actually mild. There were no real side effects except for discolored skin and a series of blue dots tattooed around her torso to make sure the beams were calibrated correctly. The daily treatments were a hassle and an annoyance for us, but after everything she had been through, they were a walk in the park. There is nothing like some unmitigated hardship to give you some much-needed perspective in life.

One night I was reading the news on my computer. Every day I read the latest news on breast cancer, praying and hoping that I would read that a cure had been developed and I would never have to worry about Carol getting sick with this ever again. To this day, I still read the news with that same hope. But that particular night, a headline from the *Los Angeles Times* caught my eye:

"Pregnant Breast Cancer Patients More Likely to Survive"

Even though the headline was simple, I had to read it a couple of times to make sure I had read it correctly. Pregnant breast cancer patients are *more* likely to survive? How was this possible? After all, one of the leading breast cancer specialists in the country had told us not one year ago that our best bet was to terminate our pregnancy because of Carol's cancer. I trembled slightly as I read the first paragraphs of the article:

There may be few pregnancy nightmares worse than finding a lump in one's breast, given the dueling fears that if it's cancer, treatment could harm the developing fetus, while delay and pregnancy hormones could fuel a tumor's growth. But a new study finds that pregnant women treated for breast cancer are more likely to survive their ordeal than breast cancer patients of the same age who were not pregnant when their cancer was diagnosed.

Five years after their diagnosis, almost 74% of the women diagnosed with breast cancer during pregnancy were still alive. Among their sisters who were not pregnant when they got treatment, 55.75% survived to the five-year mark. The researchers found some evidence that the pregnant breast cancer patients fared better on long-term survival, as well.[2]

I could hardly believe what this article was saying. Although the exact biological mechanism was unclear, pregnancy somehow fought breast cancer and significantly increased the probability of survival by 20 percent, a huge difference. This study had just been presented for the first time ever at a conference for the American Society of Clinical Oncology, its data provided by the renowned M.D. Anderson Cancer Center in Houston, Texas. Many of the best doctors in the country had been unaware of this and still believed the best course of action for a pregnant woman with breast cancer was to terminate the pregnancy and begin treatment right away, which is exactly what the specialist had advised us. No one knew that *pregnancy was actually a potent treatment against cancer*, not until this study, presented this week.

But that's not true, because someone knew—God.

We never really knew how to make sense of Carol's pregnancy. It shocked us and made us happy, but it also seemed so random. I have to admit that many times I saw her pregnancy as nothing more than a shocking and haphazard event, with no greater purpose. It was just an accident, albeit a happy one.

But in God's economy and in his wisdom, there are no accidents. It was no accident that God blessed us with this child after the last miscarriage and at that very particular moment

2. Melissa Healy, "Pregnant Breast Cancer Patients More Likely to Survive," *Los Angeles Times*, September 30, 2010, http://articles.latimes.com/2010/sep/30/news/la-heb-pregnancy-cancer-20100930.

in our lives. He knew something no one else did—no one else in the entire world. He knew this child would give us hope and purpose and the determination to persevere through the hardest moments, all of which we would sorely need. He knew the child would be born unscathed by the treatments. *And he alone knew this child was treating his own mother, mysteriously helping her physically and emotionally fight back the cancer that had invaded her body.* It had been no accident, not even from the first day we had heard. It had all been part of a mysterious and incredible plan: Jonathan would be a powerful medicine for his mommy.

I was stunned by the intricacy of it all, how the subtle but powerful hand of God could be seen throughout our story. God had given us Jonathan right at the start of Carol's treatment. He put words in the mouth of her surgeon, words with tremendous weight that gave us the courage and conviction to do the right thing. When I was talking on the phone with the doctor on the National Mall, it was God who had spoken deep into my heart, reminding me that he was up to something, and that even though I couldn't understand what that something was, I had to trust him and give his plan time to unveil itself. It was God who was the joy in my daughters' smiles, a source of such strength for Carol and me in the spring. It was God who had made sure the ultrasound reverberated with the sound of my son's heartbeat that summer. It had all been part of a divine plan, unfolding over one year.

It reminded me of a tapestry. My mother is a very creative woman, even though her life as an immigrant mother raising three children allowed her little time to express that creativity. But she loved making beautiful things, and one of the more creative endeavors she undertook was the weaving of a tapestry for my very first birthday, which hangs to this day on the wall of the house in which I grew up. I remember as a young child marveling at the tapestry, which spans seven feet by five feet and depicts a medieval-style portrait of a young woman holding a bird.

And being a curious young boy, of course I wasn't content with just looking at it but had to touch it, feel it, and eventually turn it around to see the back of it and how it was made. I was shocked to discover that in contrast to the front, the back was a mess. Long, loose threads dangled in random locations, having no discernible purpose. No picture could be seen when looking at the back of that tapestry—it was random and ugly chaos.

But then I would flip to the front again, then to the back, and then to the front, and I realized that everything I had seen in the back did have a purpose. That random blue thread was not there for nothing—it made the tiny blue dot at the center of the woman's eye. The green threads that made such a mess at the bottom were actually grass that lay beneath her feet. Every thread on the back had purposeful placement that made sense only when you looked at it from the front.

That was my life. When seen from the back, neck-deep in the trenches of painful circumstance, it was a total mess of random and accidental events that all seemed to converge in the period of one year. But when seen from the front, in light of the wisdom and timing of God, it was a beautiful tapestry, a story of hardship and suffering, but even more, of healing, providence, and blessing. Not a stitch had been wasted, not one thread without an intended purpose. Every moment, every second, every event had been woven into a stunning plan by the Master Weaver, every detail guided by the Great Physician.

But as I pondered this, I wondered if God's amazing plans and purposes were not just limited to this one year of my life. Perhaps that amazing wisdom and complexity that he had

Amy Walter Beisel

Our happy family of five (October 2010).

demonstrated was part of every year of my life, from the day I was born and even before, as was the case with Jonathan. Perhaps all the missteps of my life had been invisibly but tangibly repurposed to some amazing effect—all the seeming mistakes transformed into lessons, assets, very real blessings. And what if this revelation was not just limited to my own life, but the life of all humanity throughout all of time? Every meaningless and terrible moment given incredible positive purpose, held only in the mind and the wisdom of God and glimpsed by the fortunate, like me.

I closed my eyes and, without even thinking about it, raised my hands high above my head. I had started the night reading the news and ended it in worship, overcome by the realization that my God was like no other, that his ways truly were not like my ways. They were not simply higher—they were better.

You see, God humbled me mightily the day we found out Carol was pregnant. It was clear I would never be able to understand his ways, so I submitted myself to whatever he was doing, even if I could not begin to understand it. I could do little but throw my hands up in surrender and submission to a great and terrible God. But after Jonathan was born and Carol recovered her full health and strength, it began to dawn on me that not only were God's ways higher than my own, but they were better. God was not simply incomprehensible—he was incomprehensibly loving. I did not need to simply submit to him in deference, as if he were a king and my only duty to do and die. No, I realized that he was more like a wise father, whose purposes are too great for me to understand, but also more loving that I can ever know.

I felt reborn. Through the trials of our year—through cancer, pregnancy, church planting, and parenting—I came to know God more clearly. He was bigger to me, wiser, more loving, more powerful, able to do more than I could ever imagine. I had become a better husband to my wife. I had become a better father to my children. I had become a better pastor to my church. I saw life in general more clearly, not through the rosy but ultimately false lens of the American dream, but instead through the dream of grace through Christ—that we inevitably suffer in life but can always count on God being right beside us in the midst of it, even redeeming the most seemingly irredeemable moments.

I bounded up the stairs as quickly as I dared with three children sleeping peacefully in their rooms. Carol herself was getting ready for bed, but I halted her preparations and forced her to come downstairs with me. I led her by the hand to my computer and excitedly pointed to the screen, which she rightly interpreted to mean that I wanted her to read the article found there. As she sat down and read in silence, I watched her intently. She looked tired, which was understandable, given her treatments and the fact that she was taking care of a newborn, as well as the fact that her husband would not let her sleep. Her hair had begun to grow back, but it was different now. Her hair had always been perfectly straight but now was growing back curly, as if forever changed by everything that had transpired. But none of this mattered.

Smitten by love, I thought she looked positively beautiful.

Finally she sat back, and I could see that she too was struggling to process what she had just read, especially in light of everything we had experienced. We sat and hugged each other tightly, amazed at our amazing God. We were so relieved that our trials had come to an end, as you can imagine. But at the same time, as strange as it seems, we were glad we had gone through them in the first place. We had experienced so much and had learned so much about ourselves and about God. I asked her a tough question, a ridiculous one: "Do you think we would be as happy as we are right now if we hadn't gone through everything we have?"

She paused for a long while, stared off into the distance, and finally said, "No. No, we wouldn't be. We're so blessed."

And I had to agree. I absolutely had to agree.

Epilogue

"What About My Happy Ending?"

I t has been a few years since this all took place, and in that time I've had the opportunity to share my family's story with many people, both in writing and in person. Most people have been very encouraged by what I share and have been kind enough to tell me so. "Wow," they say, "if you can get through all that, then I think I can make it through my situation too!" I smile and nod, but then as I turn away, I wonder if that isn't some kind of oblique insult, as if they're really saying, "If THAT guy can do it, anyone should be able to, shouldn't they?"

As you can tell, witnessing a mighty work of God's salvation has had curiously little effect on my self-esteem.

But I'll never forget one encounter that unfolded very differently from all the others. I had just finished sharing my family's testimony at a church in Virginia, and afterward a woman approached me, her lips pursed tight and eyes fierce. As she drew nearer, I could almost feel displeasure emanating from her, as if I had said something terribly insulting during my talk. I racked my brain to remember if I had said any such thing or if perhaps I knew this woman from somewhere. I may not be the best public speaker in the world, but still, this wasn't the usual response I got from people. Glazed looks and snoring, sure, but not this. I braced myself for the worst.

She started by saying, "Pastor, that's a nice story."

I exhaled with relief. I had somehow misread how she was feeling and, with an overly cheery voice, replied, "Thank you! I'm glad it was a blessing. I'm sorry, but I didn't get your name . . ." She only shook her head in response, either because she didn't want to tell me or because she didn't want to be sidetracked from what she felt she had to say.

She went on. "That's a really nice story. But, you know, not everyone gets a happy ending like you did." *Okay, perhaps I had read her face correctly the first time.* Her voice trembling, she continued: "My story didn't end that way. My husband had cancer too. But he died. And because he was the only one who worked in our family, when he passed away, I had no way to provide for my two sons. The hospital bills and funeral costs destroyed us. And now? Now I'm using food stamps to feed my children. God didn't save my husband or my family. So what do you have to say to someone like me? Where's *my* happy ending?" Her eyes filled with angry tears, but she held them back, refusing to allow them to fall so as not to let her tears blunt the rage she felt inside.

My mind foundered for the right response. At first, I was tempted to subject her to a mini-sermon on what God might be teaching her through her trials. But then I thought back to those same dark moments in my own life, when feelings of betrayal and sadness wrestled for dominance of my heart, and immediately thought the better of it. I would have positively snarled at anyone who dared try to take such a condescending approach with me, and I was certain she would do the same. Instead, I told her what I myself would have most wanted to hear in those moments.

"Sister, I am so, so sorry. I can't imagine what you are going through. Tell me more about what's going on. What was your husband's name?"

She was disarmed by my response, her face hovering somewhere between anger and confusion. But then she raised her hands to cover her face, and her shoulders began to heave—gently at first, but then more deeply. And when I tentatively put my hand lightly upon her shoulder, she sobbed with all her might. Over the next hour, she told me her story in more detail. Her husband of two decades had been diagnosed with stage 4 pancreatic cancer and passed away only months later, leaving her and her two sons with little to their name. To make matters far worse, what little money they had saved was stolen from them by someone who purported to be a family friend, the worst kind of betrayal of the most vulnerable of people. I shook my head in disbelief and disgust. This woman was not exaggerating; her story had no happy ending, not even the thinnest of silver linings. I had no idea how to help her make sense of her tragic circumstances.

But toward the end of our conversation, I began to suspect she didn't even want an answer. After all, what answer could I give that would not ring absurdly hollow in the abyss that she found herself in? No, all she had wanted was to share what she was going through and how she felt, and for someone to listen. I saw her for who she really was—not an antagonistic woman who wanted to criticize me, but a brokenhearted widow and a fellow traveler on a dark road that I myself had traveled. A fellow sufferer.

When her story and sadness were finally spent, we sat quietly together for a while. At last, I said, "I'm so sorry to hear all of this. I honestly don't know what God has in store for you. But I do believe from the bottom of my heart that he does have something. Let's pray together that as hard as it might be for you to see right now, you would find the presence of God near to you during this time." So we sat in prayer for a while, and after we were done, she thanked me for my time and apologized for her initial brusqueness. I made as if I had no idea what she was talking about, which made her laugh, quite a pleasant change from her initial attitude. I'm glad to say we parted on good terms that day. But something she had said to me was lodged in my mind for weeks afterward:

"What about my happy ending?"

That was not the only time I heard that question. Quite a few people have asked me the same thing, in different ways and in varying degrees of intensity and pain. And each time they do, their words pierce me. What can I say to a person whose story did not end in the same way as my own?

First, I would have to acknowledge that I don't know.

Our story ended in a particularly miraculous fashion, where my wife emerged from treatment cancer-free and my son was born without any complications. For many, their story ends with grief and mourning that seem to have no end. And for those souls, I can do nothing but give my deepest condolences. I can't adequately explain why God chose our story to end as it did, filled with new life and hope, and don't think of myself more worthy of such an ending than anyone else. I wish everyone's story ended as ours did—I truly do.

But I would also hesitate to call it an ending at all, because that seems to imply that nothing happened after Jonathan was born, as if our lives just came to a screeching halt at that point. While Jonathan's birth was an incredible chapter of our lives, it was not the ending of our book as a whole. That story continues to be written, even now. And so it is with all of our lives; that one moment does not accurately describe the whole story God has planned for us, any more than a single snapshot can capture the entire arc of a person's life. To do such a thing, you would need many snapshots, taken in many seasons and over the course of many years.

Such an attitude is so difficult to maintain in the midst of pain or when we are overwhelmed by our circumstances. It is altogether too easy to assume that the situation we find ourselves in is our fate for all time; that is certainly how we feel at the moment, without an end in sight. But the truth is, although an individual chapter of our lives may be filled with tragedy, it does not necessarily mean that the rest of our book will end in the same way. In fact, the difficult middle chapters of our lives might do nothing more than make the true ending all the more extraordinary.

But when you think about it, the opposite is equally true. Just because one particular section of your life ends well, that hardly means you will never face hardship ever again. Take our example. A year after Jonathan was born, as a result of low attendance and dwindling financial resources, I made the difficult decision to close down our church plant. This may seem a small thing relative to everything we had endured, but it was not. The deepest experiences of my entire life were inextricably tied to that community, so it was especially heartrending to see those ties severed.

I had also hoped that if our church could survive, and even flourish, it would provide some sense of redemption and closure for everything my family and our congregation had suffered in its short life, a happy ending of sorts. But it was not to be. Although my wife would survive, as would my son, my church would not. The Riverside would be closed and disbanded, and afterward, I would be unemployed for half a year. We would be forced to find closure, community, and a job elsewhere.

Neighborhood crime also continued after Jonathan's birth. The summer after I closed down the church, my family was planning to celebrate my birthday by taking a trip to the beach, only an hour away from our home. But halfway there I got a call on my cell phone from our security company. They informed us that the back-door sensor had been tripped and wanted to verify if we were at home or not. I told them I wasn't and that they should call the police right away. I then made a U-turn in the middle of the highway and raced back home.

When we returned, three police cars were parked on the street, and officers were stationed at our front door, guns drawn. I parked the car and timidly approached the house, only to be intercepted by an officer while on my way. He told me that a K9 unit was going through the house, making sure no one was still inside. He instructed me to go across the street and wait there until they were done sweeping the home. I sat down heavily on my neighbor's front steps, glumly wondering how the thieves had gotten in and what they had taken.

After half an hour, an officer waved me over and told me it was safe to go in. As I walked through the front door, I could see that our back door had been smashed in, the door lock crushed by what I guessed was a sledgehammer. An officer from CSI was carefully dusting the frame for prints, and a large German shepherd was sniffing around in my bathroom, seemingly intrigued by what he smelled there. *This is just too surreal*, I thought to myself.

Accompanied by an officer, I wandered from room to room of the house and enumerated everything that had been stolen: some cash we had hidden, our TV and DVD player, my Xbox video game system and my favorite game (which I had been painfully close to completing), and worst of all, my wife's jewelry, including her engagement ring. The only bright spot in all of this was that before we left, for some strange reason, I decided to hide our laptops behind the sofa cushions, something I didn't normally do. And so neither of our computers was stolen in the burglary, which would have been a huge loss, as they held all of our priceless family photographs and videos. The officer called it a lucky break, and I agreed. But some part of me wondered if the Holy Spirit had led me to do this—if the Holy Spirit did things like prompt people to hide their computers behind the sofa cushions. I had never read anything to that effect in Scripture.

In the days following, my dormant fortress mentality came roaring back with a vengeance. A detective told me that most likely someone had been casing our house for a while, watching us and waiting for us to leave. This is the worst thing to tell a person who suffers from acute paranoia—that an unknown specter has been spying on them. I became convinced that people were watching us at all times, from the sidewalk, from the bus stop, and if we were to leave our home for any amount of time, it would be burglarized again. So I resolved to barricade my family inside our home from then on and never leave unless it was absolutely necessary. I might have to even engineer some moving-mannequin system around the home, à la *Home Alone*.

I told Carol this and expected her to nod in agreement. After all, it was her jewelry that had been stolen, so she must be as traumatized as I was, right? But of course she wasn't. She looked at me kindly, as she always does, but matter-of-factly replied, "Peter, I don't want to live like that. Let's go to Costco." So that's what we did. But to this day, I still hide my computer each and every time we leave the house.

So things have not exactly been "happily ever after" since Jonathan's birth, and neither is there any guarantee that ever will be the case. Since there is no cure for cancer, Carol might get sick again. Her cancer might return, in the same place or a new one, perhaps even more advanced than before. I could get sick as well, perhaps with cancer or some other ailment. Some other tragedy of a completely different sort might befall us. And just because my wife and children were saved in one particular circumstance does not mean they will never be threatened again or that I will never see difficulties in the future. I know from firsthand experience how fragile life is and that

On our way to dinner to celebrate our eighth wedding anniversary (2011).

at thirty-five, it is inevitable that I will suffer again, a prospect that frightens me.

I have come to the point where I don't believe in happy endings, at least not as they are imagined in the American media and consciousness, where all loose ends are tied, the good guy gets the girl, and everyone is better off than when they started. I have seen too much of life and walked with too many broken people to really believe in fairy tales of that sort. That's just not how life works.

Not only are happy endings unrealistic, they are deeply un-biblical. After all, there is no happy ending for so many of the heroes of Scripture, not for Paul, Peter, James, or Stephen. The final chapter of their earthly lives does not read, "But they all became rich and famous and married and lived long and healthy lives—God be praised!" No, their final chapter reads thusly: one was beheaded, the next crucified upside down, the third thrown from a building by a mob, and the last stoned to death.

No, there is no such thing as a "happily ever after" type of ending, not until Christ comes again to wipe every tear from our eyes and to make all things new. I believe very much in *that* eternal and final "happily ever after." But on this side of heaven, there is no promise we will never suffer, in the present or the future, or that life will always treat us fairly, or that we will always be victorious over our circumstances. As hard as that truth is and as loath as I am to mention it in the final chapter of this book, it is a truth we all must acknowledge and accept if we hope to deal with the reality of real life, even a real life with Christ.

So what good is it to follow God then? Do we do so only on the promise that he will provide final resolution at the end of the time, and nothing more? Can we expect nothing from him in the here and now? I don't think that's the case, because God does provide something powerful to us—no, not happy endings, but *amazing glimpses*, brief but profound moments, when we see God so clearly that it gives us just enough faith and conviction to carry on through the next valley and beyond.

That's what happened to my family and me in that pivotal year. It was not a happy ending as much as it was a brief but truly sublime glimpse into the wisdom and love of God. In that year, I witnessed firsthand that God does exist, that he loves me and has a plan, although it's a plan I never will be able to comprehend. It was just a moment in time, but a moment that sheds a bright and reassuring light on all the other circumstances I face, both currently and in the future.

No, I know I will suffer in the future, and I may not get off so easy then. But I also know—just *know*—that God will be with me, and as a result, I always have reason for hope, both for this life and the next. So no, not all of us get happy endings, but we do get amazing glimpses. And even a brief glimpse of God in the midst of the storm is better than a lifetime spent in blissful ignorance.

Perhaps one final example of an amazing glimpse from my own life:

In the fall of 2011, a year after Jonathan's birth and only a few months before the closing of the church, Carol and I were eating lunch together, Subway sandwiches. Carol is not a large person by any means, so she is usually content to eat a six-inch sandwich for a meal. But being the miser that I am, I almost always insist that she get a footlong, not because she'll eat it, but because it's a better value. "The value, Carol, think of the value!" I tell her repeatedly, to which she usually rolls her eyes.

But that day she surprisingly finished her entire footlong sandwich and then asked if I was going to finish mine. I shook my head and handed her the rest of my sub. I then watched in astonishment as my one-hundred-pound wife wolfed down my sandwich and then looked as if she could eat another one. The next morning she complained of feeling nauseated, but I knew it wasn't the eighteen inches of cheap sandwich meat she had consumed the day before. I knew what was really going on, because I had seen it three times before.

She was pregnant again.

This might not seem like a big deal, but this was not supposed to happen. I don't mean that in the sense that we weren't planning on it and were utterly shocked, although we were. I mean it was biologically improbable. Chemotherapy often induces early menopause or infertility in women, especially the specific treatment Carol received. Our doctor had told us very matter-of-factly that we weren't going to have any more children after this. But I guess God didn't get that memo, because God saw fit to let Carol get pregnant again. It just goes to show that you should never tell God what he can or cannot do in your life. I have a feeling that he views such statements as a personal challenge.

Carol gave birth to this child in the spring of 2012, another precious little girl. As with Jonathan, she gave birth to our daughter without an epidural, but this time I remembered to take off my wedding band before she went into labor. Afterward, to my great amazement, I was allowed to name this child as well and chose the name Lucy, which means "light." But I also chose this name because she is our fourth child, and the fourth child of the Pevensie family from *The Lion, the Witch and the Wardrobe* is also named Lucy. It is Lucy who asks Mr. Beaver if Aslan the Lion is safe, to which Mr. Beaver replies, "Safe? Who said anything about safe? 'Course he isn't safe. But he's good. He's the King, I tell you." That is the God I know, a God who does whatever he wants, but whatever he does is good.

Another blessed consequence of this pregnancy was the phenomenon that was described in that cancer study, that pregnancy

Katie, Jonathan, and Sophia enjoying their new sister, Lucy (June 2012).

somehow fights breast cancer and lowers the chance for re-currence. So not only did we welcome another child into our crowded home, but we were also encouraged by the fact that this pregnancy would act as a type of preventive medicine, keeping Carol's odds of recurrence even lower, just as Jonathan had done. Wow, this is like déjà vu! A miraculous child who helps support and keep its mother's cancer at bay? It's almost as if there is a plan to all of this. . . .

That is the reality of our lives. Our stories have not yet come to a conclusion; our family has since moved to the Pacific North-west, we have had *another* child, and I have begun serving at a new church. We also continue to struggle and experience hard-ship; that has not ceased, and never will until Christ comes again to make all things new, as he has promised. We will face suffering again, inevitably, and perhaps tragically. But we continue to experience blessing as well and catch powerful glimpses of God's incredibly wise and loving plan in our lives. Day by day the tapestry continues to be woven, and the story continues to be written. So I may not know what the next chapter of our life holds, but I know Who is writing it.

And because of that, I cannot wait to find out what comes next.

Carol, Katie, Jonathan, Sophia, Lucy, me, and Xavier (September 2014).

Peter Chin is a pastor, writer, speaker, and advocate for racial reconciliation. He was born and raised in the suburbs of Chicago and moved to Connecticut to attend Yale University, where he met his wife, Carol. After graduating with a degree in history, he attended Fuller Seminary and went on to pastor and plant churches in Los Angeles, Virginia, Washington, D.C., and Seattle, where he now serves as lead pastor of Rainier Avenue Church.

Peter's advocacy work in racial reconciliation has been profiled in several national news outlets, including *CBS Sunday Morning*, the *Washington Post*, and NPR's *Tell Me More* and *All Things Considered*. His essay on reconciliation between Koreans and African Americans in the inner city was one of the winners of *Christianity Today*'s "This Is Our City" essay contest.

As a writer, Peter has been a frequent contributor to both *Christianity Today* and *RELEVANT Magazine*. He is also a devotional writer for *Our Daily Journey*, a ministry of Our Daily Bread, as well as a blogger for *Christianity Today*.

Peter and Carol have five children: Sophia, Katie, Jonathan, Lucy, and Xavier. As such, Peter is perpetually tired, and perpetually thankful. For more information, visit www.peterwchin.com.